HELP!
I Want to Remodel My Home

Ann Sutherland Augustin

Help!
I Want to Remodel My Home

The New Woman's Guide to Home Improvement

Nelson-Hall **Chicago**

Library of Congress Cataloging in Publication Data

Augustin, Ann Sutherland.
    Help! I want to remodel my home.

    Includes index.
    1. Dwellings—Maintenance and repair—Amateurs'
manuals.   2. Dwellings—Remodeling—Amateurs' manuals.
I. Title.
TH4817.3A9   643'.7   74-28307
ISBN 0-88229-214-5

Manufactured in the United States of America.

To my father,
Donald A. Sutherland,
who throughout his life professed anyone could
accomplish anything
if he had faith in himself.

Contents

Preface

Has there ever been a woman who hasn't at some time looked around her and said to herself, "If only I could change this room"? Visiting a friend's new house or viewing model homes often prompts you to ask, "Why can't my home look like that?" Well, it can, and NOW IS THE TIME!

This is not a woman's lib book, but a book written by a woman for other women who wish to update their present living space to their own specifications without the outlay of a great deal of money. No interior decorator is necessary—just imagination and ideas, a fair amount of sweat, and time. Believe me, when you see the difference in your own house and know you did it yourself, then you will know the meaning of self-satisfaction.

Remember when "do-it-yourself" was a "dirty" word? It meant you didn't have the money to hire a professional. However, today's inflation has touched almost everyone. This is one reason why the do-it-yourself project is no longer the sign of a skin-flint, but is an indication of someone who knows how to budget her time, energy, and money. *Building Supply News,* a trade magazine, states that the home improvement industry expects to sell more than 8 billion dollars worth of wood paneling, ceiling and floor tiles, and other products to do-it-yourself fans this year alone.

Today, moreso than at any time in our history, many women live alone. The rising divorce rate plus the fact that the female generally outlives the male are contributing factors. But many young women are choosing to live alone. They take pride in their independence, are freed from the old pressures to "graduate, marry, have babies, and stay home," and wish to live in a place that reflects their own personality.

You might be tempted not to improve an apartment as, when you leave, the improvements stay. But you're going to lease an apartment for a year or two, why not do some minor (and inexpensive) renovations and have a dwelling to your liking? If you discuss your plans with the owner, and explain that you are going to do the work yourself, he may be more than glad to pay for the materials. After all, you are improving his property.

The greatest asset you have in home remodeling is that you will be more careful than a professional. A tradesman must lay tile, hang wallpaper, or install paneling at the fastest possible speed or he loses money on the job. True craftsmanship has almost disappeared from this country. Closely inspect a model home and you will find many flaws—tiles that do not fit tightly, quarter round that is not properly mitered (cut on an angle to insure a snug fit), and wallpaper patterns that don't quite match at the seams.

You can work at your leisure. You can start a job while the children are at school or napping and stop any time you wish. Or, if you work in an office all day, you may find it relaxing to come home and work off your frustrations on a piece of wood. It's better than hitting the boss!

Here is something that many people are not aware of. Yet it could save them a great deal of money when they purchase a brand new home. Builders often give a discount if the buyer does the wallpapering, tiling and other finishing. A builder has a certain allowance for each house to cover these items which, of course, includes the labor involved. Invariably you will find that the discount will allow you to greatly upgrade the quality of the tile and other finishing products.

I want to emphasize that, when purchasing any do-it-yourself items, you should do business with a reputable dealer. This certainly does not rule out the discount home centers (in fact, my best buys are usually made there). Know both the manufacturer and the grade of materials you are buying. Never be afraid to ask questions, no matter how stupid they seem to you. A good dealer knows that his customer's satisfaction is the greatest advertising asset he can have.

If, having purchased home improvement items, you find they do not live up to their guarantee, don't hesitate to complain. Forget about griping to the local dealer. He has too many channels to go through before you will be satisfied. Write directly to the president of the company whose product proved inferior. You can find his name by looking in the Standard & Poor's Directory of Companies (available at the library). No one wishes to be told that his product is not all it's cracked up to be. I know from personal experience that a letter sent directly to the president of a company will receive immediate attention and results.

So, to repeat, DON'T BE AFRAID TO ASK QUESTIONS and DON'T BE AFRAID TO COMPLAIN!

You are serious about wanting to remodel your house or apartment (otherwise you would not have purchased this book). Now ask yourself the following questions:

1. Would I be improving my house beyond its resale value? Any real estate agent will tell you that the most expensive home on the block is the hardest to sell. However, the improvements outlined in this book do not cost much in money. And it would be very difficult indeed to over-improve. Labor is the item that costs the most, and that you are going to supply yourself.

2. Are improvements necessary for the sale of the house? In today's mobile society, one out of every four families moves in a given year. No prospective buyer is impressed by a house with peeling paint, ripped wallpaper, or marred floor tiles. He would assume that if the surface of the house shows wear and tear, then the non-visible components (such as plumbing, hot water heater, furnace, etc.) have really been "let go." It is in your best financial interest to keep the house, no matter what its age, as up-to-date as possible.

I am not an interior decorator. Even if I were, I would not try to foist my ideas on you. Too many homes "done" by professionals do not provide for the needs or reflect the personality of the owner. Style and materials will differ depending upon whether you desire a formal home or one attuned to family living. The decision of how to remodel your home to your particular taste rests entirely upon your shoulders. All I am attempting is to show how each room can be transformed BY YOU to fit your own needs and preferences. Each step of construction will be presented in detail, but the materials you choose will reflect your own life style. I will include ideas I have used in my own homes and others that I have seen. Some of the procedures I learned the hard way (such as affixing mirror tiles to a wall). Hopefully, this book will spare you the mistakes I made.

Most home-remodeling books on the market today make the assumption that the reader already knows the correct name of each tool and its purpose. Even worse, they contain such terms as "toe-nailing" without an explanation. I have explained and illustrated the tools you will need and included a definition of the terms that may be unfamiliar to the beginner. It's time that women stop feeling that their capabilities for sprucing up their home are limited to just painting a wall. If I can do it, so can you!

I hope the following chapters will unlock a door to great satisfaction. You will be proud when you can say, "I did it myself!"

Basic Tools

Certain tools are necessary to do any home improvement project. Be sure to gather all items you need for a particular job before you begin. There is nothing more aggravating than having to get down off a ladder, or up from your knees, to hunt a particular item. Not only does tool hunting decrease your efficiency, but it's enough to drive you "bananas." So be sure to assemble all the necessary tools and materials you will need and keep them close by.

Before I go into special tools and items needed for a particular job, I will describe a basic set of tools—ones that you will use on every job and will need for minor repairs around the house. One hint: never purchase cheap tools. Not only will they give an inferior performance, but they will wear out or break much sooner than the more expensive ones. This doesn't mean you have to go "whole hog" at the store. But do buy a name-brand tool, and don't buy the cheapest of the line. Hold the tool, get the feel of it (especially necessary with a hammer), and make sure you can use it with ease.

Every basic tool chest begins with a hammer. I recommend purchasing two to begin with. The first is called a claw hammer. It has a nailing surface and a "claw" on the back (see Illustration 1). The claw is used to pull out nails. A thirteen-ounce hammer is just about right for a woman.

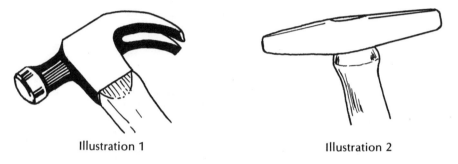

Illustration 1   Illustration 2

The second hammer for beginners is the tack hammer. It is small in size and used for small or thin nails (see Illustration 2).

Equally as important as the hammer is the screwdriver. There is probably not a room in your house that does not have screws in it somewhere. You cannot get by with just one screwdriver—you should start with at least four. There are two types of screwdrivers. One has a straight edge and is used with screws of the type shown in Illustration 3. You will need two of these, one about three-eighths of an inch wide and the other about three-sixteenths of an inch. These two sizes will handle just about any screw in your home.

The second type is called a Phillips screwdriver. It is used for screws like the one shown in Illustration 4. A

Phillips screwdriver is sold by number rather than size. You will require a No. 1 and a No. 2. There are other,

Illustration 3   Illustration 4

more specialized types of screwdrivers, but they needn't be included in your tool kit at the beginning.

You will need a minimum of two saws, although you may wish to add a hacksaw later. (A hacksaw is used for cutting metal.) Most important is a good crosscut saw, the one you probably think of when someone mentions saws (see Illustration 5). You may wish to rent a power saw for a large job, such as cutting paneling for an entire room, but you will still need a manual saw. Buy a very good one, for a cheap saw will become dull and will rip the wood rather than cut it. I prefer a saw with a wooden handle because it is more comfortable to work with than one that has a plastic handle. My hands perspire when I work and the plastic handle slips in my hand.

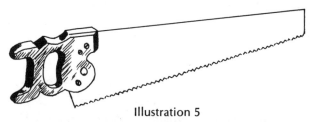

Illustration 5

The second saw necessary for most remodeling jobs is called a keyhole saw (see Illustration 6), which is intended for cutting curves or circles. If you plan to panel a room, you will need this saw for cutting the holes in the panels for the electrical outlets. Purchase one that has a six-inch blade and can be rotated into any position for ease of use.

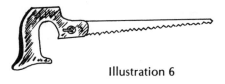

Illustration 6

You will need a drill for predrilling screw holes, installing tub sliding doors, installing kitchen cabinets, and a variety of other purposes. True, stores still sell the old-fashioned hand drill, but nothing can beat the electric type. But do not buy a cheap electric drill. Not only will it not last, but it can be downright dangerous to work with. Your choice should be a name-brand product, backed by the manufacturer's guarantee. Purchase the standard quarter-inch drill.

Pliers come next on the list. There is such a great variety offered that it is easy to become confused. Two types that are indispensible to the basic tool chest are the "slip-joint" (see Illustration 7) and the "needle-nose" (see Illustration 8).

The slip-joint pliers can be adjusted so they can grasp either small or large nuts and bolts without having the handles spread apart so far that you can't grip them. They also have "teeth" in the gripping part so they hang on to the unit being loosened or tightened, as the case may be. However, they will leave scratch marks on metal, such as a faucet, so be very careful when using them. One technique that I find useful is to wrap one layer of adhesive tape around the part to be tightened to protect the surface.

Needle-nose pliers resemble the tweezers used to

shape eyebrows, but are much larger. They are used to hold small, delicate objects. They have small tips that don't block your view of what you are doing.

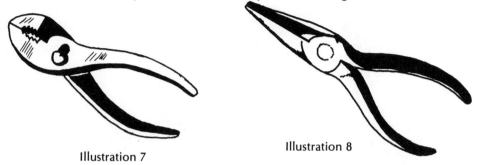

Illustration 8

Illustration 7

A set of wrenches is necessary for a basic tool kit. One type of wrench, called the "adjustable" or "crescent," can be made to fit almost any pipe, nut, or screw (see Illustration 9). A set of wrenches in various sizes, like the ones in Illustration 10, will sell for around five or six dollars. Granted, you may have to take time to find the one that fits the particular job you are undertaking, but it will enable you to do the job expertly.

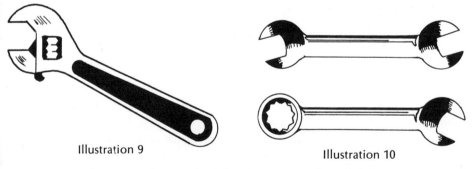

Illustration 9

Illustration 10

Almost at the end of the list comes the chisel. Originally, a chisel was used for cutting into wood. I use it in the removal of quarter rounds or base shoes (the narrow molding joining the baseboard and the floor). It also may be utilized when plastering small holes in a wall. An example of a chisel is shown in Illustration 11.

Illustration 11

I saved the best for last, but why not? It is the carpenter's level (see Illustration 12). A level is rather expensive, but is necessary in all phases of home remodeling. Don't invest in a cheap level. I have found the best level for my use to be the one manufactured by Stanley. It is a twenty-four inch one called the HANDY-MAN (No. H1297-24"). Being made of metal, it cannot warp and give inaccurate readings, as a wooden level sometimes does. The Handyman has three glass containers, each with two "bubble levels." This enables it to be used either in a vertical or horizontal position, and with either your left or right hand.

In using a level it is absolutely necessary to remember this: when the level is used in the vertical position, it is the *bottom* bubbles in the top and bottom windows that must be dead center between the lines on the glass. Do not pay any attention to the top bubbles. When the level is used in a horizontal position, the *bottom* bubble of the middle window must be centered. There are double bubbles in each window so that you can use the level in any position.

Naturally, the tools you will require depend upon the job you are undertaking. The above are just the basic

tools needed for most jobs around the house. You may
need to purchase some for a specific job you want to do;

Illustration 12

others, such as a tile cutter, will be loaned by the store
that sells you the product needed for the job, and a few
large items, such as a power saw, can be rented for a
nominal amount.

Are you going to wallpaper a room? Then you will
need a ladder. Be very sure it is sturdy enough to support
you when you reach high. Ideally, your ladder should be
tall enough so that you do not have to go higher than the
third step from the top. Not only will the ladder be less
likely to tip, but you can keep your sponge, brush, and
razor blades on the top shelf. This eliminates your having
to climb down the ladder each time you need a tool. You
will also need sharp razor blades for trimming the top
and bottom of the paper. A package of single-edge
blades will suffice for a normal-size room. The cost at a
discount store should be around seventy cents. Many
people believe they get more for their money from a
double-edge blade. This is probably true, but the danger
of accidentally cutting your fingers is not worth the
savings. And you will find that blood on wallpaper does
not lend itself to a professional look. The minute a blade
gets the least bit dull, throw it away. A dull blade will rip
the paper.

Another item you will need is a seam roller (see

Illustration 13). This is used to seal wallpaper seams after each sheet is hung. A seam roller usually sells for less than a dollar. Do not use this tool on flocked paper. It will flatten out the flock, which looks peculiar, especially under artificial light.

Illustration 13

Many people will say that a chalk line (sometimes called a plumb bob) is necessary when hanging paper. I think differently. For those who don't know what a chalk line is, I'll give a short explanation. It is a string rolled up in what resembles a fishing reel; colored chalk inside the case is deposited on the string. You can use the chalked string to make a straight line on the wall in order to hang the first sheet of paper. A chalk line, in my opinion, is almost impossible to use by yourself, unless you happen to have three hands. Once I had the bad experience of having chalk ooze out onto the paper when I rolled the seams, and I have been unable to remove this discoloration. Therefore, when I go into wallpapering, I will explain how to do this first step with a level.

You will need a hammer, a nail set, and a can of patching compound. I use vinyl spackling compound. It is already mixed and is easy to use and store. A nail set is approximately three inches long and sells for around fifty cents. It is used to countersink nails. I have learned the hard way that nails that are just beginning to pop through plasterboard walls will really show after I have put up the paper. Actually, you could use an old ice pick or an awl if you have them. However, you do run the risk of having them slip off the nail head. Dull the point with a mill file (see Illustration 14) or by pounding the point flat with a hammer. By the way, a mill file is a good investment as it is also used to sharpen other tools and cutting edges.

Illustration 14

You will need a putty knife (see Illustration 15), one that is about one inch in width. Putty knives vary in price but none are expensive. Be sure that there is some flexibility in the blade. One that will not "give" will only provide poor results. A spackle knife is identical in shape to a putty knife but is about three inches in width. This is used for repairing cracks in plaster or plasterboard. Unless you wish to own both knives, either job (repairing cracks or smoothing out nail holes) can be handled by the putty knife.

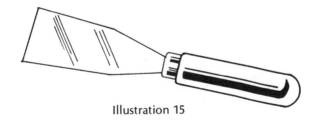

Illustration 15

Next, purchase fine sandpaper for smoothing out the spackling compound after it has hardened, and a yardstick or tape measure for measuring the wallpaper strips. I prefer a yardstick because its weight holds the paper flat on the table while you measure. Have on hand a *sharp* scissors for cutting the paper.

If you are going to use wallpaper that requires paste, you will need a paste brush. It need not be an expensive one, but before you buy it, pull on the bristles. If any come out, don't buy that brush. There is nothing more annoying than having to pick bristles off the back of freshly glued wallpaper. If you should leave one on the paper, it will show through when the wallpaper has dried. Even though you are doing the job yourself, you do not want it to look amateurish.

When you use prepasted wallpaper, you will need a water box. The plastic kind sell for around seventy-five cents. Most wallpaper stores will give you a cardboard one free when you make a purchase. You must assemble it yourself—no big deal. Just follow the instructions. The cardboard one is all right if you intend to complete the entire job in one day or if you are only doing one wall of a room. Otherwise, it has a tendency to fold in the middle after a few changes of water. And who needs water all over the floor? I am sold on the plastic water box, not only because it does not disintegrate, but also because you can use the same box over and over again and store it between jobs.

Last, but certainly not least, are the brush you will need to smooth out the wallpaper after you have hung it and a clean, wet dishcloth. I use an item called an "applicator smoother" manufactured by Product Development & Mfg. Company of Mendota, Minnesota (see Illustration 16). Its top is styrofoam, which is easy both to hold and to control. The middle layer is foam to hold water, and the bottom layer resembles a furry paint roller. This item is very inexpensive and if you buy a fairly large amount of wallpaper you may be able to talk the dealer into giving you one free.

One point to remember with this item is to keep it fairly wet, so that you do not rip the paper, but can remove the air bubbles and excess paste. The wet dish-cloth is used in the final cleaning step.

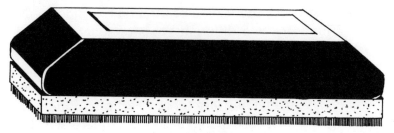

Illustration 16

Maybe you have decided to tile a floor rather than to hang wallpaper. You will still need some of the above-mentioned tools, such as a sharp scissors for cutting vinyl tile, and a good ruler. A long tape measure (the metal pull-out type) has always been considered a necessity by tile layers, as accurate measurements of the room are indispensable to a professional look. However, I find that the good old yardstick, provided it is not warped and still has both edges intact, works better for me. Since you are covering an existing floor or are working on a plywood surface, you can make your marks right on the old floor with a sharp pencil or a ballpoint pen. I find it much easier to work with three-foot units than to struggle with twelve- or fifteen-foot units.

If you do decide to invest in a pull-out ruler, buy one that is fairly wide and thick so it will lie flat. Also, get one that is twelve feet in length. One longer than this is un-wieldy and a smaller one is not so useful.

A carpenter's square is also necessary for laying tile. It is vital that the first piece be laid exactly square in the center of the area; if it's not, by the time you reach the edges of the room, the edge pieces of tile will not all be the same size. The entire pattern could very easily look lopsided. Even though you have measured the room and have used a ruler or a chalk line to make your lines, you still must check the square of the first tile laid.

There are two different types of squares. One is called the combination square. It is small and has a bubble level in the handle (see Illustration 17). This particular unit is used mainly for squaring doors and cabinets and anything else set in a vertical position. For laying floor tile, I prefer the carpenter's square (see Illustration 18). It has longer sides and enables you to draw perfectly straight lines in four directions just by rotating its position on the floor. A good carpenter's square is rather expensive, but you will find many uses for it in your home remodeling. If you don't wish to invest in a carpenter's square for a one-time job, try borrowing one from a neighbor. Most people who have done any building or remodeling have one.

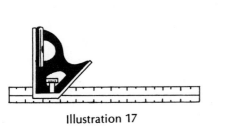

Illustration 17

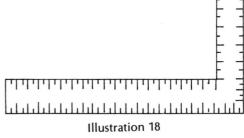

Illustration 18

If you are laying ceramic tile, you will need tile snippers and a tile cutter. Both will be lent to you by the tile dealer. Their use is explained in the section on laying ceramic tile.

Before you can lay a new floor, you will have to remove the quarter round, or base shoe (the narrow strip of wood that edges the floor on all sides of the room). More on the actual removal later; the tools you will need are a hammer and either a wide screwdriver or a chisel. You will also have to remove the existing floor or thoroughly clean it, depending on the type of new floor you wish to put down.

If you are going to lay a new floor over the existing one, you will need vinyl spackling compound and a putty knife, plus wax remover and a lot of soap and rinse water.

To remove an existing floor you will need a chisel, a hammer, and a wax stripper. The wax stripper will be used to remove the mastic (glue) that remains on the plywood after the old floor has been removed. You may even need mineral spirits, but more about that later. If there is a great deal of mastic left, as in the removal of ceramic tile, it will benefit you to rent a floor sander. Sanding will remove all the mastic, but unless the sander is used with much care, it will also remove the underlayment (the wood flooring beneath the old tile). It took making a hole in the underlayment of my front entryway to teach me this lesson

There are several different types of floors you can lay yourself. Each will be covered in a subsequent chapter. But it pays to have all tools and materials ready before you begin.

Probably the one project that do-it-yourselfers attempt most often is interior painting. Whether it is the woodwork or the walls that you decide to tackle, you will need certain items to obtain the professional look.

Most people would probably say that brushes or rollers are the essential items for painting. I am tempted to say that the drop cloth is most important. The drop cloth, or covering you will use to protect your floors, rugs, and furniture, must be of a sturdy material. We've all seen the nine-by-twelve-foot plastic sheets sold in paint and variety stores. Forget them. In this case, a penny saved is absolutely not a penny earned. In fact, the cost of repairing the damage done when a thin plastic piece rips may far exceed the cost of buying a good drop cloth in the first place.

The best drop cloth is one made of heavy muslin. These are expensive, running around twenty dollars. You can make one yourself if you have a sewing machine. Heavy unbleached muslin can be purchased at most discount stores for under a dollar a yard. If the muslin is thirty-six inches wide you will need sixteen yards to make a drop cloth twelve feet by twelve feet. Cut the sixteen yards of muslin into four lengths of four yards each (twelve feet). Sew the four pieces together (see Illustration 19) and you have a drop cloth that will last for years. If you have pinking shears, pink the rough edges. If not, forget them. The little bit of raveling won't amount to anything.

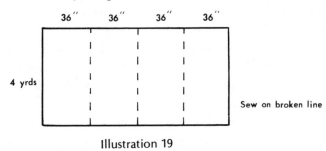

Illustration 19

If you've ever had the experience of trying to open a gummy plastic sheet or of getting paint on the plastic and then having it stick to your shoes so that you track it through your house, then you realize why a fabric drop cloth is so important. After all, paint belongs on the wall and trim, not on the carpet or furniture. So either buy or make a good drop cloth; don't purchase one that is going to "die" during its first hour of life.

Now, what brushes will you need? Since there is no chapter on painting, I will briefly go over the essentials. The day of using brushes on the walls and ceilings is almost over. Even professional painters have, for the most part, given them up. Rollers now do as good a job as any brush, if not better. But be sure to purchase the correct roller for the job you are undertaking. The same roller will not do every job in the house. Some rollers are made for latex paints, some are designed for flat paint. Others are produced for oil-base paints and some are made for stucco or cement walls. A reliable paint dealer will be able to advise you on the roller you will need.

One thing that I will emphasize, however, is that when you buy a paint roller, purchase a unit of good quality that allows for slipping the roller on and off. You will be saving money in the long run, as you can use the roller handle over and over again by just replacing the cylinder according to the desired job. If you do not want to clean the roller, you can buy a replacement for the next job, since new rollers are not expensive. Just keep in mind what a professional painter would charge to paint a room, and you'll see what I mean.

For painting around the ceiling or wall edge I use an edge trimmer (see Illustration 20). It has small wheels (or rollers) on top that ride along the ceiling and it prevents an overlap of paint onto the adjoining surface. It also has replaceable pads so you can use the cover unit over and over by just replacing the pad. The cost of the entire unit is less than two dollars. It will pay for itself many times over, not only in time saved but also in the neatly painted edge it will achieve.

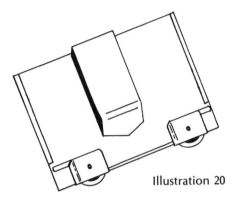

Illustration 20

You will need a paint brush for trim (the wood or metal around the doors and at the base of the wall) and for the window sashes (the edging surrounding the window glass) and frames. I remember being told as a youngster that there was no brush as good as a natural bristle brush. Having now used both natural and synthetic bristle brushes, I really do not see much difference in them, save the price. The synthetic ones cost quite a bit less. But a good synthetic brush will do an excellent job—remember, good, not cheap! In fact, with latex paints I have found that the natural bristles soften too much. Why, I cannot tell you, but it does happen.

Please, don't buy cheap brushes. Not only do they drop their bristles all over your work, but they give a very uneven coverage. You will have to spend many more minutes dipping the brush into the paint, because a cheap brush does not "hold" paint. Remember, although you're trying to save money, you are also going to conserve time.

For painting trim or moldings there is a fantastic item available that eliminates the problem of paint getting on the surrounding wall. It resembles a curved ruler with a handle on top (see Illustration 21). By laying it against the wall you are able to paint the trim without painting the wall. Just remember to wipe it after making each brush stroke (great use for old shirts—you can wipe it on yourself).

Illustration 21

When you are painting, keep rags nearby at all times. Wipe up any spills immediately! A damp rag will clean up latex paint spills and one slightly moistened with turpentine will clean up oil-base paint. Do not wait until you have finished the entire room and then try to clean up any paint that has splattered on the woodwork. Remember good paint is made to dry and stick. It is easy to ruin woodwork by trying to remove dry paint.

Laying Ceramic Tile

    This chapter will be devoted to instructions for laying ceramic tile. However, your choice might be marbelized vinyl tile or imitation slate. If you decide on any form of vinyl or vinyl asbestos tile, follow the directions for laying vinyl flooring found in a later chapter. The directions for laying imitation slate ceramic tile are the same as those for regular ceramic tile. And, of course, the same directions apply regardless of which room you are tiling.

    Probably there is no other area in your home that is more important than your foyer, or entryway, whether it is very small or immense. Pretend you're a guest entering your house. Open the front door and really see it for the first time. Is the entryway too small or, as in the case of many ranch homes, is it missing altogether? Is it a large entry, but one that looks like nothing more than a hallway connecting rooms? You can correct these problems easily

Let's begin by deciding how large an area you want in your foyer. In some cases, the layout of the house will automatically determine this. If, as in the case of many bilevels, the entryway runs directly from the front door to the kitchen, then this will be the area you will tile. Contrary to what many interior decorators may say, you will not be visually cutting down the size of the living area by tiling a foyer. In fact, the contrast in materials used will make your entryway appear larger and will define your living room.

Most ceramic tile sold today has a gauzelike backing on the sheets. This is not to be removed. It keeps the tiles in the correct pattern arrangement while you are laying them and also helps them adhere. A small number of manufacturers still sell their tile with brown paper on the face of the tile. This brown paper is also left in place while laying the tile.

There are two drawbacks to tile that has its face covered. The most important one is that if one of the tiles is defective or is not correctly positioned on the paper, you will not be able to tell. By the time the tile has set and you have removed the paper, it is too late to do anything about it.

Secondly, removing the paper is a hassle. You have to soak the paper thoroughly with warm water, loosen it, and then scrub and scrape it off. This is no small job and, to say the least, a messy one that you would be well advised to avoid. Small bits of the paper which get stuck between the tiles must be removed either with your fingernails or with a small screwdriver or knife before you can fill in the spaces with grout. Water will also accumulate in these spaces, and you must allow them to dry thoroughly before grouting (laying the colored pastelike cement between the tiles). Otherwise, the grout will become too thin from excess water. Try to avoid using tile that has brown paper on its face.

It has been my experience that ceramic tile with a high factory-applied gloss just can't be beat. Cold water cleans it perfectly, and any spots wipe up with a damp cloth. Mop it once a week, and people will think you slave over it every day. Having four teen-agers and three dogs, I think I can speak from experience. However, this type of tile is slippery when wet.

Ceramic tile is one of the easiest tiles to install, but one of the most expensive to have installed by a professional, due to the extra time consumed by the cutting and grouting processes. Even if you make a slight mistake with ceramic tile, it is almost impossible to see it when the job is completed.

Tile comes in several sizes. I prefer a small pattern in a small entryway. Not only is it easier to lay in a confined area, but it will have the tendency to make the foyer look bigger. A large and busy pattern may destroy the illusion of space you are trying to create, and by the time you have done all the necessary cutting and fitting, you may very well have lost the beauty of the pattern. Today there are many mosaic tiles that are suitable for an entryway or a bathroom. Check with your supplier to make sure that the pattern you have chosen will be able to take the constant wear and tear it will be subject to. Some mosaic is made strictly for tables and counter tops and will scratch and crack when walked on. I would like to stress the importance of dealing with reputable dealers. They will be honest in explaining the advantages and disadvantages of certain tiles.

After you have decided on the brand and pattern of tile you want, shop around for the best price. Don't let anyone talk you into an inferior product by saying that it will accomplish the same results. Buy top grade materials. They are easier to work with, and the results will be professional and lasting.

For a wide foyer, or one that extends from the front of the house to the rear, try one of the large patterns. They come in different shapes and are most impressive, especially when laid with a contrasting grout. Some even are sold with pieces that are already cut in half for laying around the wall edges. This saves you the time and effort of cutting these pieces. But if the pattern you choose does not offer these half sections, don't be dismayed. It is not hard to cut ceramic tile when you have the proper tools. Just remember to borrow a tile cutter and snippers from the dealer when you buy your tile.

At least one company that I know of manufactures a ceramic tile that is pregrouted. It can be used on either the floor or the walls. The sheets are two feet by two feet and each tile is one inch square. I have never used pregrouted tile, so I can't really give the pros and cons of using it. However, the idea is good since there would be no grouting to do with the exception of around any fixtures (as in a bathroom) or where the tile meets the wall. Pregrouted tile would naturally be more expensive. But if you dislike the mess of grouting and have the money to spend, perhaps you would want to look further into this kind of tile.

I put down one hundred eighty-five square feet of white ceramic tile in an entryway that has eleven doors or openings. Because I chose a tile that had eight points (octagon shaped) I had quite a bit of cutting to do. Granted, my hand hurt for a few days, but the end result was well worth it. The point I'm trying to make is that you do not have to stick with square tiles, unless they happen to be your preference. Don't shy away from the odd-shaped ones.

Most do-it-yourself manuals probably tell you to measure the area to be tiled before you choose your tile pattern. I find that when I do this, I have a tendency to choose tile by cost rather than because I like it. Since you will save a tremendous amount of money by installing the tile yourself, you may as well pick the tile that will bring you many years of pleasure.

Once you have chosen your tile, go back home and measure the area to be covered. Most ceramic tile is sold by the sheet, which usually measures twelve inches by twelve inches (one square foot). Take your tape measure, or yardstick, and measure the length in feet of the area you wish to tile. Write that down. Now measure the width of the area in feet and write that down. Multiply the width by the length. For example, if your foyer is seven feet wide by ten feet long you will require seventy square feet of tile (seven times ten equals seventy).

Don't forget to add on for any closets you wish to tile. You would also be well advised to buy at least three or four extra sheets to keep on hand in case replacement is necessary at a later date.

Using the above formula you can figure out fairly closely how much tile you will require. Naturally, if there are many cuts to be made, you will need extra tile, since you have a greater waste factor. But by taking time in deciding the placement of the tile you can eliminate part of this waste and also some of the cutting.

You will find that you will utilize cut-off pieces that a professional installer would automatically throw away as he cannot afford the time to cut and file leftovers.

Now, take your measurements back to the dealer. He will also figure out how much tile you need. His amount and yours should not differ too much. If they do, check both sets of figures carefully. Some dealers automatically add on five percent to cover cutting and waste.

Be sure to have your dealer guarantee that you can return any tile that you do not need or that is defective while it is still on the sheet. For double protection, have the dealer write this down on the bill of sale. This will prevent any haggling if you should return some sheets.

Now you have chosen your tile, have determined the amount you need, and are ready to bring it home. The dealer will sell you the correct mastic (glue). With a little bit of talking on your part you may be able to get him to throw in (for free) a trowel. The trowel is the tool (see Illustration 22) you will need to spread the mastic. A small, tin, disposable one will not do a good job. Hold out for a heavier one that has a wooden handle and serrated edges with two sizes of teeth. A trowel can be used over and over if you clean it with turpentine, paint remover, or even hot water after each use.

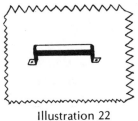

Illustration 22

The directions on the mastic can will tell you whether to use the small (one-eighth inch) teeth or the larger side (one-fourth inch teeth). I find that smaller teeth do a better job. You will have enough mastic on the floor to hold the tile, but you will not have an excess that will come up through the spaces between the tiles, thus making grouting difficult. As grout is a form of cement, it also holds down the tile.

Now for the preliminary steps to laying tile. You will have to remove the quarter round or the base shoe. These are small pieces of wood that lie directly on the flooring where the floor meets the wall. Don't confuse these pieces with the baseboard. The baseboard is the larger piece of wood that runs up your wall. It is absolutely not necessary to remove this. In fact, to do so would destroy your wall. Some houses do not have a baseboard or base shoe. If you have such a house, purchase either quarter round or base shoe and install it after the tile is laid. This covers the cut edges for a finished look. There are many ways to remove the quarter round or base shoe. Some people merely rip it off, thus destroying it. Not only is this a waste of money, but when you replace it you have to stain the new piece to exactly match the baseboard—not an easy task. Others remove the nails, but since they are usually countersunk, it is difficult to get at them. To place each nail into its correct hole when reattaching the piece takes too much time, but if you make new holes, you have to putty and stain the old ones.

It has been my experience that if you start at one corner of the room with a hammer and screwdriver and work carefully, you can remove the quarter round and later replace it, and there shouldn't be a mark on the wood to show it has been removed.

Take your screwdriver, one with a thin head, or your chisel, and gently insert it between the quarter round (or base shoe) and the baseboard. In some cases—if the wood has been painted many times or is too tightly affixed to the baseboard for a screwdriver to be inserted—you can use a putty knife. Tap the handle of the screwdriver (or putty knife) with the hammer, just enough to remove the quarter round from the baseboard about one-quarter of an inch. Now move down the quarter round three or four inches. Repeat the above procedure. Repeat it until you have reached the end of the piece. The nails will still be in the wood and won't be bent out of shape. Pry this piece loose from the baseboard, using either the screwdriver, a chisel, or your fingers.

Turn the piece over and, using a marking pen, make a number 1. You then will know this was the first piece taken off. When the time comes to replace the quarter round, line up the nails in the wood strip with the nail holes in the baseboard and hammer them back in place. Be sure to use a nail set so you will not make any marks on the quarter round.

Repeat the above procedure with each piece of quarter round, marking them as you take them off with numbers 2, 3, and so on. When you are ready to replace them, they will go on easily and you will not have any touch-up to do. In fact, no one will ever be able to tell you removed them—unless you wish to brag about a job well done!

You will also have to remove the metal thresholds. These are the anodized gold or silver strips of metal that are installed on the floor where tile meets another material, as in an archway of a dining room or a living room. They are used to cover the rough cut edge of a tile and the turned-under piece of carpeting or the cut end of a wood floor. To remove them all you need is a screwdriver. Just unscrew the screws in the threshold and it will lift right off. Be sure to mark the back of the metal with a number so you will know which piece belongs where when you have to replace them.

One last thought on metal thresholds. Sometimes the ones that are installed in your house are marred or scratched. To reuse these will detract from the new look you wish to achieve. You may wish to change from gold to silver, or vice versa. Lumber and hardware stores stock thresholds. They are not expensive and can be installed after the tiling job is completed with a minimum amount of labor.

If you choose to purchase new thresholds be sure that you measure the width that you need very carefully. You can always shorten the length by cutting off a piece with a hacksaw. But the width must be sufficient to cover the rough edges of both materials where they meet. Metal thresholds are sold in different shapes. You will need a threshold that has one side higher than the other if you are installing it in an opening where tile meets wood. The tile is higher (due to its thickness) than the wood flooring. Other thresholds are almost flat. Again, rely on the advice of a reputable dealer. He will be able to tell you which type best suits your particular need.

Bring along the dimensions of the thresholds you need when you talk to your dealer. He will be able to cut them to size for you. But be absolutely sure of your measurements. Nothing will detract more from your new tile floor than to have a threshold that is too short. That is a sign of a careless amateur.

You will have to remove the existing floor, unless you are working with a wood floor. Even if the present flooring is vinyl or vinyl asbestos, the very thickness of ceramic tile precludes laying it over the vinyl. After all, you don't want to step up or down into your foyer. Also, the metal threshold may not lie correctly when there is a large difference in the floor levels of two rooms.

Removing the old flooring is not that hard, but it is time consuming. If you don't think it is worth your time, just call a tile installer and ask him what he would charge to remove the floor. You will be floored! So the hours you spend are money in your pocket, not to mention the satisfaction you will feel in a job that you have done entirely by yourself.

Right now you probably have one of three

coverings in your entryway—carpeting, vinyl tile, or ceramic tile. Each must be removed in a different way.

Let's start with the easiest—carpeting. If the area you plan to tile is not bounded by walls, you will have to decide where to cut the carpeting. The threshold will cover and secure the cut edges when you turn them under. Cut your carpet so that it extends about one inch over the area you will be tiling. For example, to tile an area four feet by four feet, cut out an area that measures three feet, eleven inches by three feet, eleven inches. This allows the raw edge of the carpet to be turned under to prevent raveling.

If at all possible try to plan your cut so that you can use whole tiles or sheets of tile. In other words, if you are using tile that comes on twelve-by-twelve-inch sheets, try not to make your area four feet long by four feet four inches in width. You will then have to cut tiles to fill in the extra four inches. Granted, you may still have to cut around any door openings, but the fewer the number of cuts the better the job will appear.

Carpeting may be installed with tacks. If your carpet has visible tacks, remove them with the claw side of your hammer. It may be necessary to insert a screwdriver under the tack to pry it up enough so you can grasp it with the hammer claw.

If your carpet was installed tackless (a misnomer in my mind, since nails are pounded into your floor that leave much larger holes than tacks), you can easily pull the carpeting loose from around the wall area. However, when you remove the carpeting you will find a narrow piece of wood nailed to the floor. This is what has been holding down the "tackless" carpeting. This strip of wood must be removed with a hammer and chisel. Nail holes will be left in the floor. If you are installing ceramic tile, it is not necessary to fill the holes. The mastic you use will sink into them and the tile will make them indiscernible. But if you intend to lay vinyl or vinyl asbestos, these holes must be filled in with putty. That step is covered in the chapter on laying resilient (vinyl) flooring.

The second type of floor that you may have to remove is asbestos, vinyl asbestos, or solid vinyl tile. I wish I could come up with an easier way to remove it than with hammer and chisel, but I can't. Some builders do not use much mastic, so after you have chiseled up one or two pieces of flooring, you can almost pull the others up by hand.

There is one other trick I learned that enables you to remove this tile easily, but you must be very, very careful. If you have a heat lamp, direct it for a minute or two—no longer—on the tiles to be removed. The heat will soften the tiles and the mastic, thereby allowing easier removal. But always remember that an improperly used heat lamp can start a fire. Do not use it when small children are present, because they may be tempted to touch it. Do not put the heat lamp down on the floor without turning it off. These common mistakes can turn an ordinary home improvement job into a tragedy. So unless you are prepared to take precautions with a heat lamp, stick with the hammer and chisel.

Ceramic tile is removed the same way as vinyl tile, except that a heat lamp won't help you one bit. Only good old pounding and chipping will do the job.

After the old tile is removed, you will find quite a bit of the mastic stuck to the underlayment (plywood or hardwood floor). Most of it you can pull off with your fingernails, assuming you don't care if you lose part of a nail here or there. After all, who has ever seen a carpenter or tile setter with beautiful long nails?

There are three ways of removing leftover mastic.

Let's start with the easiest. Buy a can of quality wax stripper. Use according to the manufacturer's directions, but let it stay on the floor for a minimum of fifteen minutes, preferably longer. You will find that the mastic will be loosened sufficiently for you to remove it with little trouble. Let me stress that it is necessary that all the old mastic be removed before you begin to lay a new floor. Otherwise you will end up with an uneven floor or, even worse, one that will crack when pressure is exerted upon it.

If the above process does not remove all the mastic, you must proceed to step two. But let me say I have never found it necessary to resort to this. This is a dangerous procedure because of the fire hazard. You will be using mineral spirits, a highly combustible substance. Suffice it to say that you do not smoke when using mineral spirits. The directions on the can will emphasize this. But it is also vitally necessary that you turn off all pilot lights in the vicinity. Open the windows and doors so that fresh air is circulating throughout the room. So what if it is a little cold—that's a lot better than starting a fire!

Use the mineral spirits in just a small area (three feet by three feet) at one time. Clean and rinse that section before going on to the next section. You are protecting yourself and your home by working in small areas rather than tackling an entire room at one time.

The third step in removing old mastic is sanding. I found this was necessary when I removed old ceramic tile in our foyer in order to replace it with new. Ceramic tile requires a different type of mastic than other tiles, a type that is more difficult to remove. I had to rent a sander and sand off the old mastic. Renting a sander is not expensive, but what a messy job I did! Although I was sanding the entryway, the dust went into the living room, dining room, kitchen, and den. So if you do have to resort to sanding a floor, learn from my mistake. Take down the drapes in every room adjoining the work area. Cover all the furniture in those rooms. Most important, keep your vacuum cleaner right with you. Vacuum up the mastic dust immediately. You'll save yourself hours of clean-up time when the sanding is completed.

The final preparatory step is to vacuum the entire floor and wet mop it to remove every last particle of mastic or dust.

Now for the first and most important step in the actual laying of the tile. You must determine the starting point, and the intersecting lines which determine it must form four right angles. Otherwise, when you reach the corners of the room, the tile pattern will be uneven and your floor will look terrible. But it is not difficult to find the correct starting point (see Illustration 23).

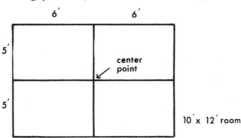

Illustration 24

You will need a tape measure (steel) or a yardstick, and a sharp pencil or a ballpoint pen. Measure the width of the room (from one wall to the wall directly opposite it). You will come up with a figure in feet and inches. Divide this figure in half to find the center of the width of the room. Make an "X" mark at that place on the floor. Move to one end of the room and repeat the above procedure. Then do it again at the other end. You now have three center points marked on the floor. By making three separate measurements you compensate for any wall that is not perfectly straight (and very few are).

Join these marks with a straight line. You can use a chalk line for this, snapping it across all three marks on the floor. Although I will not recommend a chalk line for wallpapering, it is all right to use one for marking a straight line on a floor. After you have made the center marks on the floor, fasten down the chalk line to the first mark (the one nearest the wall) with Scotch tape. Pull it snugly across the middle mark and tape it down again on the last mark on the floor. Go back to the middle "X" and lift the string with your fingers about three inches off the floor. Then let it snap back into place, taking care that it hits the center "X." Your line should be perfectly straight (see Illustration 24). On a small floor area, I sometimes use a heavy steel tape measure and a ballpoint pen instead of a chalk line. The end result is the same.

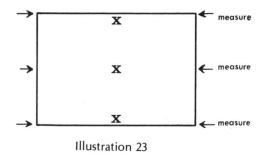

Illustration 23

Now measure the length of your room, using the same procedure outlined above. You will now have a giant cross on the floor. Where the lines intersect is technically where you lay that first, and most important, tile (see Illustration 23).

I say "technically" because sometimes by using the

dead center as your starting point you will end up having a wider margin of cut tile along the edge of the floor at one side of the room than you will have along the opposite side. For example, you might have to cut four inches off the tile on one side of the room and six inches off the opposite side. You are better off moving your "center" line over one inch towards the larger tile. This way you will cut five inches off the tile on each side and thus have even borders. Check both length and width in this manner and make any adjustments in your "center" line right now (see Illustration 25).

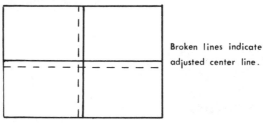

Broken lines indicate adjusted center line.

Illustration 25

Now lay a loose line of tiles following the straight lines on the floor. Do it in both directions (length and width). This is a double check on your measurements. (See Illustration 26.) Remember, you can always move that center line an inch or so in either direction so that the end cuts are almost equal in size, which is what gives a professional looking job. In fact, more than professional, because most tile men will not take the time to insure that the edges are identical in size.

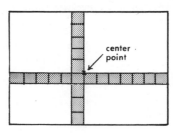

center point

Illustration 26

You now have center lines marked in both directions. Whether or not you have changed that center starting point, you now will need your carpenter's square. Put it on the floor where the two lines intersect, with the inside corner of the "L" on the crossing point (see Illustration 27). The inside edges of the carpenter's square and your lines should be in alignment. If not, you're going to have to remeasure and make new lines or adjust the existing ones.

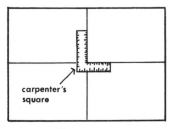

carpenter's square

Illustration 27

Open your mastic can—it's time to start laying the tile. I find it helps to use a stick (such as painters use to stir paint) to remove the mastic from the can. The trowel probably won't fit into the can anyway. Even if it does, it will get full of gook that will stick to the handle and to your hand. Try to keep the handle free of any mastic. Otherwise you will find that the handle will stick to your hand and pull the skin. You'll have one sore palm!

The floor is marked off into four sections. Spread your mastic, using the trowel, over one section (see Illustration 28). However, if you are going to have to cut end tiles, do not spread the entire area with the mastic. It will only solidify before you have made the cuts, and you will then have to remove the hardened mastic. Stop about one-quarter of an inch away from the last (furthest out) full tile to be laid. When you press down on the tile, the mastic will spread. If it spreads beyond the last tile and solidifies, you will end up with a lump of mastic that will have to be scraped loose, or the adjoining piece will not lie flat.

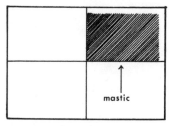

mastic

Illustration 28

Check the directions on the can of mastic you purchased. Some will say you can lay the tile immediately. Others will tell you to spread the mastic and wait, in some cases up to half an hour, until it gets tacky (meaning you can touch it and it won't come off). Follow the directions to the letter. Otherwise you will not get good results. Not only will you be disappointed, but you will have wasted your time and money and possibly the tile.

Lay the first sheet of tile (or single large tile), lining it up exactly on the two cross lines you made when determining your starting point (see Illustration 29). Now, as an added insurance against being off center, lay your carpenter's square alongside the tile and see that it is snug along both sides of the square. Now you can press this first, and most important, piece into place. The hardest part of the job is now finished.

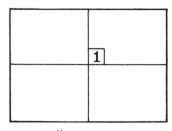

Illustration 29

Following Illustration 30, lay down piece number two. Line it up with one side against the straight line on the floor and the bottom side directly *above* tile number one. Not only must it lie against the vertical line you have drawn, but it also has to fit against the horizontal edge of tile or sheet number one. I don't want to make this sound difficult. If you have lined up your sheets vertically (lengthwise), then the horizontal (width) should automatically fall into place. But do check to see that the pattern is running straight. Now lay tile sheets number three and four according to Illustration 31. STOP!

Stand back and look. Does the tile look straight to you? No reason why it shouldn't if you have followed directions, but you will want to step back and check after each four or five tiles or sheets have been laid. Sometimes when one works too close to a pattern one cannot see mistakes. Even a defective tile (and you will find some in any batch no matter how much you paid for it) may not show when you are on your knees. But when you stand up and survey the floor, you will be able to see any defects and can either remove the faulty tile, replacing it with one from another sheet, or move the entire sheet into the correct position while the mastic is still pliable (wet enough that the tile can be moved). If you remove a tile from another whole sheet, set this incomplete sheet aside. Don't throw it away. You can utilize it when you come to the cutting that must be done around the edges of the room.

Now, complete laying the tile in the first quarter of the room, leaving the edges, if they need cut tiles, until the room is completed (see Illustration 31).

Repeat the entire procedure in the second, third, and fourth quarters of the room, remembering always to work both out and up rather than in only one direction. You have now completed the floor except for the

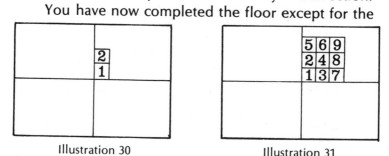

Illustration 30   Illustration 31

cut pieces that must go around the edges (if this is necessary in your particular room). That really wasn't so difficult, was it? In fact, you may find it hard not to show off your new floor right now. But wait until it's finished. Your halo will really shine!

You have borrowed a tile cutter and a tile snipper. With a little bit of luck and assuming you took care in the original measuring, doing the edges shouldn't be difficult. In order to make the edge cuts it is necessary to cut the correct number of tiles needed for each length off a full sheet. Make one cut, leaving the backing intact. You can use one side of the sheet, then turn it around and use the other side, thereby making each sheet suffice for two lengths (see Illustration 32). Should you have to cut any individual tiles to make them fit at the very edge, remove those pieces from the backing and cut individually.

12″

↕ 3″ ←— edge piece

12″ | throw away

↕ 3″ ←— edge piece

Illustration 32

Be sure, when cutting edge tiles, that you follow the

pattern that is already laid. In other words, the tile that you are going to cut must match up with the tile sheet laid right next to it. With perfectly square tile, or tiles that have an odd shape but are still of equal size, you won't have any problem matching the pattern. But if you have chosen tile that has squares, rectangles, or ovals of different sizes, it is absolutely imperative that you follow the pattern as it was laid out on full sheets by the manufacturer.

In cutting edge tile, I find it easier to cut a number of tiles at one time. This way I don't have to stop after each cut to spread mastic and lay one piece. But be sure to mark the tiles on the back with numbers (1, 2, 3, etc.); then you will know instantly where each piece is to go when you are ready to lay them. Using your marking pen, write the corresponding number directly on the floor. This way, it is impossible to get confused. When you are ready to put on the mastic, lay your tiles out in front of you in the order of their numbers and the numbers you have written on the floor. Put the mastic on the back of the tiles and stick them in place. No mix-ups this way.

The dealer will explain to you how to use the tile cutter. Because each brand is operated slightly differently from the next, it would be impossible for me to cover each individual one. You will find all types easy to operate.

Don't try to cut the edge pieces so that they fit tight to the baseboard. It is better to leave a small (one-quarter inch or so) gap between the tile and the wall. There are two reasons for this. First, it will enable you to move the tile so that you have the same space between it and the other tiles as occurs on the manufacturer's sheets. Second, it will allow the grout to seep between the tile and the wall. This creates a watertight seal. When you replace the quarter round you have taken off, the mastic and any mistakes you have made in cutting the tile will be hidden. You will need to purchase and install base shoe or quarter round if it was not previously on the wall. Nail it to the wall, not to the tile.

Don't start with a corner piece when cutting tile. Start one tile over from the corner, and continue across the width of the room. Stop before the next corner cut. Continue down the adjoining wall. Stop at that corner and finish the remaining walls. Perhaps many tile setters would not agree with me, but I have found I can do a more exact job if I leave the corners until last. By doing the sides of the room first you are assured that they are lined up perfectly with the sheets of tile already cemented in place. Cutting the corners requires a double cut, and it is very easy to make one cut either too large or too small, thus throwing off the rest of the pattern.

To cut tiles for the corners of the room or to fit around the door jambs (frames), use your tile snippers. They resemble a wide toenail clipper. Earlier I stated that usually you can borrow tile snippers from your tile dealer, but if you purchase your tile from a discount house, you may have to buy snippers. However, tile snippers are not expensive. Once you have laid ceramic tile and see how easy it is, you will find many more places where you will want to install it. Having your own tile snippers is not a bad investment, as you will probably use them over and over. But be sure to purchase good ones. Cheap tile snippers will dull almost immediately and will crack and chip the tile, thus ruining it and wasting your time and money.

When clipping corner tiles to fit, don't try to make

the entire cut in one or two operations. You will be cutting two edges of one piece of tile and it is all too easy to crack the tile if you try to make a fit in two snips. Make small snips, just chipping away a little bit at a time until you have made your corner piece the desired size. A tile wasted is time and money wasted. So be sure to take your time.

As stated before, the quarter round or base shoe will cover the edges along the walls, but around a door frame there is no quarter round. So you must be very accurate when cutting these pieces. That is why it is so important to take small snips and to lay the tiles in place first without mastic to be sure they fit properly. Once you are satisfied with the fit, spread the mastic on the back of the tile. You would find it difficult if not impossible to lay the mastic on the floor because you are working in such a small area. Do not put too much mastic on the tile. It will spread when the tile is pressed into place and you certainly do not want mastic to ooze up between the tiles or onto the wall.

All the tile is now laid. Doesn't it look great? One final inspection—squat down and look at the surface, keeping your feet flat on the tile. Have you gotten any mastic on the face (top) of the tile? Everyone does, so don't worry. But get it off immediately! Turpentine will do it. Or follow the directions on the back of the mastic can for removing any excess. Do be careful when you walk on the tile. It can easily move under pressure. That's why I recommend squatting rather than kneeling. It isn't the most ladylike position, but there will be much less chance of moving the tile. If you kneel on newly laid ceramic tile, your knees will move the tile, and the spacing for the grout will be uneven. Anyway, squatting is good for the figure, and that's an added bonus for any woman (or man).

Also remove any excess mastic that has oozed up between the tiles. A thin knife will do the job. Just take care that you do not move the tiles.

You have checked your tile for correct placement and replaced any defective tile (whether it be chipped or uneven in size). You have cleaned up any of the mastic that has gotten on the face of the tile. Now it's time to quit for awhile. By this time, you need a rest. But more important, so does the tile. Let it rest (and set) for at least twenty-four hours before spreading the grout. Try to keep everyone off it if possible. I would suggest waiting forty-eight hours. Besides, you'll probably need two days to get your muscles back in shape!

Once the tile is set in the mastic, you can walk and kneel all over it without moving it. And in order to grout you will have to kneel on it. Be very sure the tile is solid on the floor before you begin grouting. Probably the most important reason for letting the tile set thoroughly before grouting is to give the mastic time to dry. As the mastic dries, it shrinks. The mastic must shrink as much as it is going to shrink in order for the grout to completely fill in each space between the tiles. So don't be impatient. Let it set.

You probably purchased the grout at the same time you purchased your tile. But did you look at all the different colors of grout that are available? It used to be that you were limited to off-white or dark grey (which was called black). Today, because of the use of pigments, you can have almost any color you wish. Black or white tile can be striking when used with red grout. Pale green tile could be set off with dark blue grouting. The color combination may be limited by the surrounding areas (as in a small entry opening directly into another room) or may be as bold as you desire. Be sure to ask the dealer to show you all the colors that are available in grout.

The front entry in my house is done in white ceramic tile, and I chose black grout because the wallpaper is red and white and the stairs are carpeted in red. The contrast is striking. The point to remember is this: If you are tiling in beige, don't feel you have to use beige grout unless you really want it. Try deep brown. Don't grout white tile with white grout. The effect of the tile will be lost. Tile must be noticed to be appreciated, and only by contrast will your tile stand out.

Spreading the grout is easy, but it is also messy. I find it pays to spend a few cents at a discount store for a small plastic pail. Mix the grout in this pail. Grout, which is really a form of cement, gets heavy when mixed with water. A light-weight plastic pail is easy to move as you work. You'll also need another pail (or two, if you don't want to stop and change the water too often) filled with clear rinse water, and a sponge to wipe excess grout off the face of the tile. Don't use a rag to wipe up the excess grout as it will remove the grout from between the tiles.

The directions for mixing grout with water are on the bag. I have found it advisable to use a little more water than is called for. True, the grout will take longer to dry, but the results will be far more satisfactory. The grout must sink completely into the spaces between the tiles and totally fill them. If you make the grout too thick, it will not sink down to the old floor (underlayment material). Thus, when it dries and shrinks, you will find that some grout is below tile surface level. Or, the grout will develop holes in it due to the settling. Once grout has hardened, you will find it almost impossible to lay new grout in holes or depressions. New grout does not adhere (stick) to existing grout. So mix it a mite thinner than the directions say and be sure it runs into every space between the tiles and also between the edge tiles and the baseboard.

When applying grout, start in a corner of the room. Spread the mixture heavily. I cannot emphasize this enough. Only by putting on much more than you need will you be absolutely sure that the grout is sinking down to the floor level and filling every space between the tiles. Try to work within a four-foot-by-four-foot area at one time. Otherwise, you are going to be kneeling in the grout.

I have found that the best way to spread grout is with my fingers. If you do this, make sure you wear rubber gloves because grout stains. Your fingers will do a good job of pressing in the grout while still keeping it level with the tile top.

Now is the time for the sponge and the bucket(s) of clean, cold water. Let the grout sink in, but don't let it sit too long on the face of the tile. Using a flat sponge, start wiping the excess off, remembering to rinse the sponge often in the clear water. Also, remember to keep the grout even with the tile. Do not insert the sponge between the tiles. When the water gets dirty, change it! Rather than flushing it down the toilet, walk out your front door and pour it alongside the curb in the street.

If there are unusually large spaces between the tiles, you may wish to use the handle of a toothbrush to give a slightly concave look to the grout. Or you can use your thumbnail if you don't mind grinding it down slightly. I find that when grout is depressed below the tile, it becomes a great dirt and dust catcher, thereby making cleaning chores that much greater. But some people do like the look of curved grout, especially when the tiles are solid twelve-inch squares or larger and have exceptionally large spaces between them.

Keep spreading the grout, remembering to rinse with clear water as you go along. You'll be amazed at how quickly this procedure is accomplished. One final mopping with a sponge mop and cool water the next day will remove any grout that may still be adhering to the tile face.

Earlier in the chapter I explained how to remove the quarter round or base shoe. Now is the time to replace it. Since you left all the nails in place and marked the pieces in the order of removal, it is a simple job to replace them. Simply start with the piece marked number 1. Line up the nails with the existing holes in the baseboard and hammer them in—but not all the way. It is all too easy to hit the quarter round with the hammer and make a mark or a dent in it that will need repair. Use your nail set for sinking the nails. Place the nail set on top of the nail and hit it with the hammer. You cannot make a mistake, although you may hit your fingers. But a bruised hand will heal; it's much harder to correct a dent in the wood.

You will also have to replace the thresholds. If you are using the old ones, simply screw them back in place. If you purchased new ones, you probably will need to make new holes in the floor. If you don't have a drill, you can start the hole with a nail. Place the threshold across the opening and, using a pencil, mark the floor where the screws are to go by tracing through the holes in the metal. Start the hole (not through the ceramic tile, but through the adjoining floor) by pounding a nail about one-quarter to three-eighths of an inch into the floor. Remove the nail, put the threshold in place, and you will have no trouble putting in the screws that hold the threshold in position.

You're done! Stand back and be proud. You did it all yourself!

Hanging Wallpaper

Once you have installed a new ceramic tile floor, you will be amazed at how dingy the rest of the immediate area looks. So you'll probably want to redo the walls. If you intend to lay a new floor, regardless of type, but haven't gotten to it yet, do so before you hang wallpaper or paint the walls. When laying floor tile you often have to lean against the wall. This is especially true when laying vinyl or vinyl asbestos tiles. With vinyl tiles it is easier to lean against the wall and push the end tiles into place with your feet than to pull the tiles toward you with your fingers.

Just remember to cover your new floor with a drop sheet (paint cloth).

Before you start on the walls, take a good look at the ceiling. It will undoubtedly need painting. Paint it before you paper. This way you can drip a little paint on the walls and it really won't matter. As a matter of fact, unless there is wallpaper already on the wall (that you will need to remove), paint not only to the edge of the ceiling, but also down the wall about one-half inch. The paint helps the wallpaper to adhere better and will minimize any mistakes you might make in cutting the wallpaper. Who wants to see the old color peeking through at the ceiling level when you have freshly painted the ceiling and hung new wallpaper?

There is one big exception to the above. If you are using gloss or semigloss enamel on the ceiling, don't let any run down the walls. Wallpaper does not adhere to enamel paint (more on that later).

Some people prefer to wallpaper both the walls and the ceilings of a room. My opinion is that the size of the room determines this. Keep in mind also the size of the pattern you have chosen for your wallpaper. A small room can look more spacious if you choose a small pattern or a vertical stripe. Were you to pick an extremely large pattern, it could very well become overwhelming in a small space.

You can wallpaper the backs of doors, so decide whether you want to do this or to have the contrast.

In wallpapering either a bathroom or a kitchen, it is *very* important that the paper you choose be not only washable (to my way of thinking, a misleading term), but scrubbable. This is especially true in kitchens. Even with stove hoods (exhaust fans over the burners) in the kitchen, grease accumulates on the ceiling and walls. I would suggest one of the new "shiny vinyl" papers. They are extremely easy to clean.

It is probable that you will want to paint or refinish the woodwork in the room you are papering. If so, be sure to do it before hanging the wallpaper. Again, this need not take much time because you don't have to be very neat. When you paint the ceiling, you paint down the walls one-half inch or so. Do the same if you are painting the trim. There is nothing more annoying to the eye than a gap between the trim color and the wallpaper. If you trim the paper too short the gap won't be too noticeable if it's painted like the trim. However, if you need to remove existing paper, do it before you paint the trim. If you have baseboard heating ducts in your home, paint them now also.

It is possible to paper over existing wallpaper, but you probably won't be satisfied with the results. If the original paper begins to peel, then the new paper will come right off with the old. Probably most of us have lived in old homes or apartments that have layer upon layer of paper on the walls. The bumps and seams are noticeable, and should water leak behind the wall, God help you! So if there is existing paper on the walls, I certainly suggest you take the time to remove it. Actually, this is not anywhere near as hard as it sounds.

Most of the wallpaper sold today is strippable. This means all you need to do to remove the paper is to open one seam at the base (bottom) of the wall with your fingernail (notice how we keep losing those nails!), get a grip on it, and pull it up. For some reason I have never been able to fathom, it is far easier to pull the paper off the wall from the bottom up than from the top down.

Even if the original paper has been put on with paste and is not called strippable, you usually can pull most of it off by hand. My neighbor was going to repaper her bathroom and planned to rent a wallpaper remover. I said, "Let me try pulling it off." The paper had been hung by her husband with paste and was not the strippable kind. Yet, in fifteen minutes I was able to remove most of it. I say "most of it" because there were small patches that would not come off by pulling. However, my neighbor did not have to rent a wallpaper remover, but was able to remove the last pieces by soaking a sponge in hot water and thoroughly wetting the paper. This loosened the paste enough so removal was easy.

There are times when you will need to rent a wallpaper remover. If there are many layers of paper on the walls, a wallpaper remover will save so much time it will be worth the price of the rental. Most rented removers use steam to soften the paste to make removal of the paper easier. These machines are not difficult to operate. But first try removing the paper by hand. This takes more labor, but it does save you money.

If you feel you must rent a wallpaper remover, ask the person from whom you rent it for exact directions on how to use it. Steam can burn you badly. Be sure you use the machine safely and carefully.

Before you resort to rental, try hot water and a sponge, soaking the paper thoroughly. Sometimes adding a little bit of wallpaper remover (sold in wallpaper or paint stores) to the water will do the trick.

Now that you have removed any existing wallpaper and have painted the ceiling, trim, baseboard, and heater units, you are ready for the last few preliminary steps before you hang that beautiful new paper.

If the walls you intend to wallpaper have enamel paint on them, it is absolutely necessary to remove the high sheen. Don't bother using a commercial paint remover. It is messy, takes too much time, and is unnecessary for this particular job. Using sandpaper and a lot of "elbow grease," you can take the high finish off the walls in a minimum of time. It is not necessary to remove all the paint. Just be sure to remove the gloss. Use a coarse grade sandpaper and rub the entire wall area. This does not take much time because rough sandpaper will remove the gloss easily. After sandpapering, go over the walls with a damp cloth. This removes the dust that has accumulated and allows you to see any spots you may have missed. If you missed any spots, take care of them now. Then take a fine grade sandpaper (0000) and lightly sand the entire wall, smoothing out any lumps or chips. I have found that if I wrap the sandpaper around a block of wood or a common brick, it is much easier to handle. There are professional sanding units sold, but if you can make your own, you are that much ahead.

After the final sandpapering is done, wipe down the entire wall area with a damp cloth, as you did after the rough sanding job. You must remove all dust particles. Even the smallest imperfection in the wall surface will be discernible when the paper is hung.

Whether you have plaster walls or plasterboard walls, you will no doubt have to make some minor repairs in them before papering. If you have plaster walls you will need to get out your spackle compound and your putty knife. Look closely for any cracks. Check especially where the ceiling meets the wall. Cracks have a tendency to appear there. Fill in all cracks with the spackle compound. Let the spackle dry to allow for shrinking. You'll then have to apply another coat of spackle. Smooth out the wet second coat with the putty knife, making it as even with the wall as you possibly can. After this coat has thoroughly dried, you will need to sandpaper it smooth (use 0000 grade). These may seem like tedious steps, but they are necessary for a professional look. Also, they are the steps that many so-called professional wallpaper hangers will skip in an effort to get the job done faster.

Many newer homes have plasterboard walls. I don't

intend to debate the merits of plasterboard and plaster walls. However, preparing plasterboard walls for papering entails different steps than preparing plain plaster walls.

Walls that are plasterboard consist of sheets of board that are attached with nails to the studs. These nails and the seams where two boards meet are then covered with tape, and the tape is sanded smooth (if the job is well done). However, even in the best taping jobs you will find nails that have popped through. Even though they don't come entirely out of the wall, they are still noticeable. So you must countersink (drive below wall level) the nails. To do this, you need a nail set and a hammer.

To countersink each nail, place the nail set on the head of the nail and hit it with the hammer. Make sure the nails are depressed into the wall. This is important because you don't want them to reappear under the wallpaper. Following the same instructions given above for repairing cracks in plaster, fill in the holes where the nails have been countersunk. Also, repair any cracks in the wall itself, again following the method for repairing cracks in plaster.

The walls of some homes, especially older ones, have a rough surface commonly called sand finish or light stucco. If you wish to paper walls finished like this, you must remove the rough surface. To hire a professional to smooth it out would cost a small fortune. You can do it yourself with a small piece of concrete or brick.

Take the piece of concrete or brick in your hand and rub the wall surface. The idea is to take off the rough edges and protruding stucco. You will create a lot of dust, but the sand finish will come off easily. Use ready-mixed gypsum board cement to cover any indentations.

This product is sold at any building supplies store or lumberyard. It adheres to paint and is much easier to use than finishing plaster.

Using a putty knife, cover the walls with a smooth coat of gypsum board cement. Apply the cement so thinly that the paint on the walls still shows through. All you wish to accomplish is to fill all indents and make the wall fairly smooth. I say "fairly smooth" because your next step is to sandpaper the surface with a medium-grade paper to remove any remaining imperfections.

After sandpapering, wipe the walls with a wet cloth to remove any cement dust. Having done this, you must seal the walls with a commercial sealer. It is possible to make your own sealer with equal amounts of fresh shellac and denatured alcohol. (I figure that I save enough money doing everything else so I can afford to purchase a commercial brand of sealer instead of mixing my own.) Any wall that has not been previously painted must be sealed before papering. If it has been necessary to make extensive spackle repairs, then the repaired area, too, must be sealed before papering. Otherwise, the paper will not adhere to the wall. (Actually, it is a good idea to seal any spackle that you have applied.)

With the exception of a stucco wall, you can seal any wall with paint you have around the house (as long as the paint is other than semigloss or high gloss). Just slap the paint on the repaired parts and let it dry. The walls are then sealed, and the paper will adhere.

Now that you have completed all preliminary steps for wallpapering, you are ready to measure the walls and to purchase and hang your wallpaper. On to the essentials.

Perhaps you are planning to wallpaper that foyer you just tiled. Or maybe you wish to paper your living room, dining room, or a bedroom. The technique is the same for any room. Only the layout will differ.

You might wish to paper only one wall. That is what I did in our girls' bedrooms, and they were free to hang pictures, posters, and other teen-age keepsakes on the other three walls.

One other thought before I get down to the business of papering. If you are planning to paint and paper your children's rooms and they are old enough to take an interest, let them pick out their own color scheme and paper. You'll be amazed at how they will reflect their own personalities in their choices. And, best of all, they will take better care of the room because it's theirs.

My older daughter chose a yellow and green flower print wallpaper for one wall and yellow paint for the three remaining walls. The younger girl wanted a wallpaper with black and white "smile faces" for one wall, lavender for the three other walls, and a deep purple carpet. The boys didn't want paper because they wished to cover their walls with gigantic posters and newspaper cutouts. At first, I was taken aback by the choices, but the final effect is pleasing and truly their own. And all the children take care to keep their rooms looking good.

Once you have completed all the preliminary steps outlined in the previous chapter, it is time to choose your paper. First, however, you must measure the wall, or walls, that you wish to cover.

Standard walls are eight feet in height. But be sure to check your particular walls. Then measure the width of the wall(s). Also, count any doors or windows in the room since they will decrease the amount of paper needed. The exception to this is if you wish to paper the doors. Then don't subtract them. Take rough measurements of the windows so you will know how much less paper you require. Write this information down and take it to your dealer.

If you are wallpapering a stairway, the paper drop (how long a sheet you will need) may well be eighteen feet from the first stair step to the ceiling on the second floor. As you proceed up the stairs the sheets will be shorter in length. In determining the amount of paper needed for a stairway, remember that a stairway does not conform to the usual eight-foot room height.

There is one other very important point to remember in deciding the amount of paper needed—the repeat of the pattern. If the paper you have chosen has a very small pattern (or one that does not need matching, such as a vertical stripe), then you will not need much extra paper. However, if you have picked a paper with a large pattern, you will have to allow for waste in cutting the paper so that each sheet exactly matches the one next to it. I have seen model homes where the paper does not match at each seam, a sure sign of shoddy workmanship. You should be able to put a level across the pattern throughout the room and never see a deviation in the bubble. This is professional work, and this is what you are going to achieve.

Wallpaper is generally sold in double rolls. Offhand, I can think of only one company that still sells single rolls. A double roll averages seventy-two square feet. This does not mean you will get seventy-two running feet of paper. "Square feet" takes into account the width of the paper. Some wallpaper is fifteen inches wide, some eighteen, and some comes in other widths.

To roughly figure the amount of paper you require for each wall area, multiply the height of the wall by the width. This gives you the number of square feet in the wall. Subtract the square feet of any windows and also that of any doors that you do not intend to paper. Divide this figure by seventy-two (the number of square feet in a double roll of paper). This will give you a fairly close idea of how many rolls you will require for each wall.

Each roll of wallpaper has a dye lot and a run number. Make sure that the paper you buy all has the same lot and run numbers. This means that the entire batch was produced at one time, and has a uniform color. This is one reason I recommend buying one double roll more than you actually need. If you spoil a piece (and, believe me, it's very easy to do), you may never be able to purchase another roll from the same run. This is especially true if the paper had to be ordered for you. The difference in the color or match of a different dye lot or run number may be quite noticeable. Sometimes the width of the paper also varies in different runs. Another reason for purchasing more than you actually need for the job is that if one sheet of paper should get damaged in the ensuing years, you can easily replace it. So buy an extra roll and store it away from heat and dampness; then you will be prepared to replace one or more sheets of wallpaper in an emergency. When a water leak stained one wall in my house, I was most grateful that I could replace the ruined paper with paper from the original run.

You'll need only a rough idea of how much paper you will require because all dealers have a chart that will tell you exactly how much paper you will need. But it's always a good idea to have your own figures in case of a great discrepancy between your estimate and that of the dealer.

Most people have a discount wallpaper store in their vicinity. It is well worth your time and money to shop there. When I papered our entryway, I saw the paper I wanted at the local paint store for $8.50 a roll. I was able to purchase the same pattern by the same manufacturer at the discount store for $6.40 a roll. I needed twenty-two double rolls, so this resulted in quite a savings. There is one other point in favor of stores that specialize in wallpaper. They have many more books and patterns to choose from than does a paint store that has to stock a variety of different products.

There are two types of paper from which you must make a choice. One is prepasted and the other needs to be pasted. My own preference is the prepasted. It is so much easier and less messy to hang than the type you have to spread paste on.

Another choice you must make is between paper that is edge trimmed (called pretrimmed) and paper that is not. Although you certainly can work much faster with a pretrimmed paper (meaning that the rough edge on either side has been removed), don't shy away from paper that is not if it has the pattern you want. Many papers are sold in this manner (not pretrimmed) to protect the butting lengths against curling, denting, or tearing.

Removing the protective edge is a simple procedure. You will see small perforations about one inch in from the edge of the roll. Simply rap (sharply) the perforation line against the edge of a counter top. Rap the entire circle to loosen it and you will be able to remove the edge with no trouble. Do not unwind this piece—just snap it off with the palm of your hand. Use the same technique you use when you open the round cardboard container of refrigerated dough for rolls. If you are afraid to try it yourself, ask the dealer to do it for you.

Occasionally, on a roll of paper that is not pretrimmed, you may find only a line on the front of the paper showing you where you are to cut off the edge. No need to rent a machine for this. Lay the paper flat on a table, and line up the marks with a carpenter's square. Before you begin to cut, put many layers of newspaper beneath the wallpaper. You don't want to cut into your table. Use a very sharp razor blade and slice the paper, using the straight edge of the carpenter's square as your guide. Trim only one sheet (one length) at a time.

Paper that is pretrimmed does not need the above procedures. It is ready to be hung when you bring it home.

There is a continuing controversy about which is better: prepasted wallpaper or wallpaper that needs to be pasted. I have already stated my preference: prepasted. It has been my experience that it is much easier for one person to hang the prepasted type, since all that is necessary is to unroll the sheet from the water box and slide it onto the wall. However, pasting paper is not really difficult, so choose the paper according to pattern and the effect you wish to convey.

Some people will say that paper you paste yourself will adhere better than prepasted paper. All the paper in our home is prepasted, and none has, as yet, peeled. I have seen flocked paper that was pasted by the person hanging it, and the results are very poor. The paste oozed out between the seams and discolored the flocking. The more the paste was washed off, the worse the damage to the flock became. It flattened out and, due to the washing necessary to remove the excess paste, the color is much different at the seams than in the center of the strip.

Now to begin. Gather all your tools before you start: a ladder (unless you are seven feet tall), scissors, a ruler, a level, a pencil, razor blades, a seam roller, a wet Applicator Smoother (shown in the tool section), a dishcloth, spackle, a putty knife, and a bucket of clean water. If you have a wallpaper brush, by all means use it. If not, the Applicator Smoother will do as good a job, if not better. If you are using prepasted paper, you will need a water bucket.

Before you even think of cutting that first sheet of wallpaper, you must mark a straight vertical line on the wall on which you are going to line up that very important first sheet. If this piece is not hung exactly plumb (straight), subsequent sheets will get further and further out of line. By the time you reach a corner of the room or a door opening, the slant of the pattern will be very noticeable. So take your time and make sure that the original line is perfectly straight from floor to ceiling.

Now you need to determine where to make that important line. Never start in the corner of the room. Nine times out of ten you will find that the corners are not exactly straight. (This is why I always wrap the corners with the paper, but more about that later.) Also, try to put the first sheet on the least noticeable area of the wall. The pattern may not match at the juncture of the first and last sheets. Measure the width of your paper. If it is eighteen inches, make a mark at the top of the wall about fourteen inches from the corner of the room (see Illustration 33). This will allow you to turn the corner with the paper. If your paper is other than eighteen inches wide, subtract four inches from the width. Use this measure-

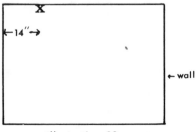

Illustration 33

ment in determining how far out from the corner to make the line.

As I mentioned previously, some people prefer to use a chalk line to mark the vertical line. To use the chalk line, tack or Scotch tape the end of the line at the point where the ceiling, the wall, and your predetermined starting point meet. Let the chalk line hang down the wall, but lock the unit so the line ends one inch above floor level. It will swing until it stops in the vertical position. Then take another piece of tape and secure the line to the wall near the floor, being very careful not to move the string. Stand back, take the chalk line in your hand at its center, and snap it against the wall. The line is now set. Check it with your level to make sure it is perfectly straight. Use the level in the vertical position and run it along the chalk line. If the chalk line is off, make corrections according to the bubbles in the level.

Because of the messiness of the chalk line, I make my vertical line with the level alone. Simply begin at the ceiling, at the mark you have determined as your starting point. Put your level in the vertical position. Line it up with the mark on the outside of the level and make sure the bubbles are dead center in the windows. Lightly run a sharp pencil along the edge of the level. Move the level down and repeat the above procedure, until you reach

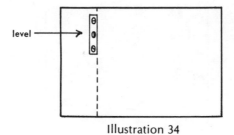

Illustration 34

the bottom of the wall. You now have a straight line, with none of the mess of chalk (see Illustration 34).

Now cut your first sheet of paper. This takes longer than the next cuts because you want to be sure that the pattern will be hung on the wall exactly to your liking. Is there one line, flower, or design on the paper that you think would make a nice border along the ceiling? Then cut your paper accordingly. Examine the paper you have chosen and try, if possible, to have a complete pattern starting at the ceiling. With some papers this is not possible due to the intertwining of the pattern. But do choose a ceiling line that is pleasing to your eye.

You have already measured the height of your wall. Do not cut the sheet to this exact measurement. You must add on at least two inches—one inch that you will temporarily affix to the ceiling and another inch that you will stick to the baseboard, or lay on the floor if there is no baseboard. This is absolutely necessary since the walls in a room are not exactly the same all along their length. You will cut off the excess with a razor blade. If you chose a particular pattern to edge the ceiling, be sure to add the extra inch above the pattern.

When you purchase the wallpaper, the dealer will tell you the repeat. If the repeat is large (eighteen inches in my entryway), you need more paper, and you will have more wastage. But don't throw away those cut-offs! They will come in handy when you paper above a door or window—assuming, of course, that the pattern matches. If you are wallpapering an entryway that has a stairway, you may be able to use some of these cut-offs to paper below the first three or four stairs that face the entryway.

Cut your second sheet of paper before you hang the first strip. Using a table or the floor, lay your first sheet next to the remainder of the roll. Match the pattern perfectly, taking care to match flowers with stems that may be on the adjoining piece. This way you are assured that the patterns will line up perfectly. Cut the second sheet. It is not necessary to measure any further strips—just cut them the same length as the first.

Always keep the last piece of wallpaper cut as the pattern for the next in line. Before you cut the third sheet, hang the first. This will enable you to tell if you have placed the border, if there is one, where you want it. If you are not pleased with the border, all you have wasted is two sheets. After you have hung three or four sheets, checking each vertical edge with the level to be sure the sheet is hanging perfectly straight, you can cut three or more sheets in succession. This saves time in cutting and hanging. When you cut quite a few pieces at one time, be very sure to mark them on the back with a pencil indicating the order in which you are going to hang them. Mark the back of the first piece 1, the second 2, and so forth. Remember always to keep the last cut sheet on the table to use for matching the pattern for the next piece.

Now comes the actual hanging.

Let's start with wallpaper that needs to be pasted. When you purchase the paper from the dealer, he will recommend the correct paste for the job. Wallpaper paste comes in powder form. Mix it according to the directions on the package, using a lightweight plastic pail. You'll need a large paint brush to spread the paste onto the paper. Put one sheet of paper, pattern side down, on your table and spread it with the paste. Don't apply the paste too thickly. It will only ooze out through the seams and make a mess. Check for lumps of paste that may adhere to the back of the paper (if you take your time in the mixing, there should be no lumps). If there are any, remove them now. It is next to impossible to smooth out lumps when the paper is on the wall.

After spreading the paste, fold the sheet into thirds (see Illustration 35) with the pasted sides together. When I say "fold," I don't mean crease! A sharp crease line in wallpaper will never come out. By gently folding the paper into thirds, you will avoid any creases and also will not have to try to work with one long sheet.

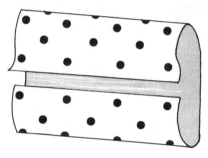

Illustration 35

The top third of the piece is opened first; this is the section with the surplus that will adhere to the ceiling (that important one inch). Open the top third and lay it directly against the vertical line you have drawn on the wall. Position it to the right of the line. (Working to the left would entail turning the corner, and this requires a little more patience and experience. When it comes time to go around a corner, you'll be such an expert that you won't have any problem at all.)

Don't forget that you may wish a certain pattern to follow the ceiling line. If so, place your paper accordingly. In any event, be sure to leave that very important one inch that will temporarily adhere to the ceiling.

Using your Applicator Smoother, smooth the paper outward from the vertical line and upward. You will probably find it necessary to pull the paper away from the wall (especially near the ceiling) from time to time in order to smooth it perfectly. Do this only on the *right* edge of the paper, never on the side resting against the vertical line. This is perfectly permissible because it not only keeps the paper in alignment with the vertical line on the wall but also keeps the pattern as straight as possible across the ceiling line. I say "as straight as possible" because few ceilings, regardless of the cost of the home, are perfectly mated with the walls beneath them.

Now, unfold the bottom third of the paper. Let it hang freely—it usually won't dry out in the short time necessary to finish hanging this sheet. However, if it should, just spread a little paste directly on the wall where necessary. Following the same instructions as for the first third of the sheet, hang the remainder, remembering to smooth the paper outwards from the vertical line and always being sure that the left edge of the paper remains directly on the straight line. Again, you may find it necessary to loosen the top of the paper in order to smooth out the entire sheet. Don't worry about it. It will restick in most cases. If not, just spread some paste directly on the wall.

After hanging this first, and most important, sheet, stop, step back from the wall, and really look at it. Is the sheet hung perfectly straight along the vertical line you drew on the wall? Are there absolutely no bulges or lumps in the paper? Have you smoothed it out completely with your Applicator Smoother or damp cloth? One hint: *small* air pockets can be eliminated by puncturing them with a fine pin and then lightly rubbing the paper with a wet cloth.

It is vital that the first sheet of paper be hung absolutely perfectly. If the first sheet is off center or bulging in any place, the following sheets will not be straight. So take great care with the first sheet and the rest will almost hang themselves.

To double check, lay the level along the right side of the paper, sliding it down the wall to the paper's end. Check those bubbles and see that they are centered. If your vertical line was drawn accurately, this side will present no problems. Should the bubbles be off, recheck that first piece *immediately.*

After you have made sure the paper is in the position you want it, run the seam roller along both edges of the paper, making sure to overlap onto the wall. This will seal the paper to the wall so there will be no chance of its pulling loose at the seams. You will notice that excess paste will ooze out. Using a wet cloth, wipe this paste off the wall immediately. If this paste is allowed to dry, you will have trouble when you hang the next sheet. It will not butt up tightly to the previous one. There is nothing more annoying than having to sandpaper spots of paste off a wall when you are in the process of hanging paper.

Do not use a seam roller on flocked paper because it will flatten out the flock. Instead, use the Applicator Smoother, keeping it very wet. Seal the edges by running the Applicator Smoother in the direction going against the nap while applying pressure on the seam. This way you will not flatten the flocking.

When that first sheet is hung, it's time to hang the next piece. You have already cut it so that the pattern matches. Follow the previous instructions, but take great care that you match the preceding sheet when affixing it to the wall. So many of the patterns have part of a design on one sheet and its corresponding part on the next that you must be careful. But if you have cut the pieces as I specified (using one as the pattern for the next), you should have no problems.

After each sheet is hung, check it with your level as you did the first sheet. Sure, it takes time, but it's worth it. Don't hurry the job—you'll only botch it up.

Now that the first few sheets are hung, it's time to use the razor blade. Some people use a brush to define the line where the ceiling meets the wall (by pushing it firmly into the groove). I prefer to use my fingernails (see, there go those nails again!). Using your nails will make a very definite edge, and you will find it much easier to cut away the excess accurately.

Run your fingernail along the juncture of the wall and the ceiling. Should there be any imperfections in the wall, your hand will easily detect them, and you will not make an improper cut into the paper.

The same procedure works where the wallpaper meets the baseboard or floor. Again, use your nails to push the paper into the space between the wall and the baseboard. If the paper meets the floor, run your nail right along the edge of the floor. This way you will have a definite cutting line.

I find the paper will cut far more easily if I let it dry somewhat before I cut it. Wet paper has a tendency to shred and rip when cut. I usually hang two or three sheets and then go back to the first piece and do the trimming. Don't wait until the paper is totally dry or you will have to scrape it off the ceiling and baseboard.

When trimming paper start an inch or two from the left seam. Don't start at one edge. It is all too easy for the paper to rip or pull away from the wall. Pull your razor blade in a straight continuous line (following the indentations you have made with your fingernails) from left to right. Stop at the seam edge of the next sheet. Reverse the procedure to free the remaining inches. Pull the excess pieces free from both the ceiling and the baseboard. Take your wet cloth (clean) and wash off the paste on the ceiling and the baseboard or floor. Again using your fingernails, seal the paper tightly behind the baseboard. With a wet cloth, press the paper snugly against the ceiling line, and also along the floor if there is no baseboard.

This procedure is also used when the paper must be cut around a door opening or a window frame. Use a sharp razor blade; a dull blade will rip your paper.

When preparing a sheet to paper above a door or above and below a window, it is vital that you remember one thing: even though you are going to shorten the length for the opening, you will need the full width of the sheet above and below the window frame and above the door (see Illustrations 36 and 37). Don't make the mistake of assuming that because there are only three or four inches between the last wallpaper sheet hung and the frame you can use a cut-off. Were you to do this, you would lose the continuity of the pattern.

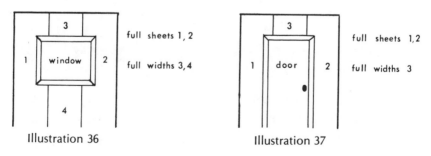

Illustration 36   Illustration 37

However, you can utilize cut-off pieces, if they are the full width (but short length), above a door opening—not down the side—or above or beneath a large window. But you must be very sure that the pattern matches the sheet next to it.

Sometimes, in this situation, I make a rough estimate of how much paper is going to be cut out for the opening, and then I cut this amount out of the sheet before pasting the paper. This makes the sheet easier to handle. If you choose to follow this method, be sure to allow for the overlap on the ceiling and baseboard but, more important, allow yourself at *least* three extra inches on the area next to the frame. You'll be surprised how often those extra inches are "eaten up" when you butt the paper tightly to the previous sheet and fit it around the frame or opening.

Every room has at least four inside corners. (An inside corner is where one wall meets another making an L.) In contrast is the outside corner (see Illustrations 38 and 39). An outside corner usually is used to cover a stud (the piece of wood that holds up the ceiling). Both are treated somewhat the same when it comes to hanging paper.

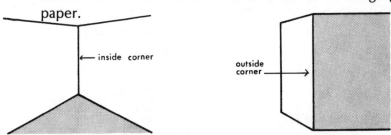

Illustration 38   Illustration 39

Let's start with the inside corner. There are different opinions on how to treat an inside corner. Some people recommend that you cut the sheet of wallpaper when you reach a corner and start with a new piece on the adjoining wall. I do not subscribe to that method.

First of all, most corners are not even and straight. Therefore, I find it difficult to exactly match the cut edge of a sheet of paper to another sheet of cut paper. Second, the continuity of the pattern is destroyed if you do not match the corners exactly. If you cut one sheet, in order to match the pattern you will have to cut the other. You surely don't want one-half of a flower ending up in the corner and an entire flower adjoining it. This will give the project an amateurish look, and this is exactly what you want to avoid. I did *one* corner of my dining room by the above method, and found it difficult. But, as I said before, you can profit by my mistakes.

My preference is to "wrap" the corners. This takes a bit more time than cutting, but the final results are worth the extra trouble. You will end up with one continuous line of unbroken pattern around the entire room and the effect is most pleasing to the eye.

Before you decide which way you wish to handle the corners, look at how it was done in other people's homes. If you choose to cut at each corner, be sure to use a sharp razor blade and to perfectly match the pattern with that of the adjoining wall.

Wrapping an inside corner can be somewhat tricky, but with the right tools it certainly isn't difficult. You will need your level and, perhaps, the spackle compound plus the putty knife.

Check the corners carefully for any obvious indents. These must be filled in with spackle. Should there be a bulge in the corner, chip it out with the chisel, and then smooth it with spackle. A good way to check on the straightness of the corner is to run your level down it. Is the bubble way off center? Then either fill in with spackle or chisel out the lump, as the case may be. One hint: it is far easier to spread spackle than it is to chisel out plaster or plasterboard. I certainly advise correcting an uneven corner with spackle rather than resorting to the chisel. Let the spackle dry before applying the paper.

Take the sheet of paper that is to go around the inside corner. Paste it or wet it, as the case may be. Fit it tightly to the adjoining piece already on the wall. Line up your pattern exactly, and press the paper into place. Now, using either the wallpaper brush (if you purchased one) or the edge of your hand, press the paper firmly into the corner. If you do not force it all the way into the corner, the paper will not adhere to the wall, and it will rip at the slightest pressure.

You will find it necessary to make a cut into the piece that temporarily extends onto the ceiling. Otherwise, you will not be able to turn the corner perfectly. This cut is similar to the one done when turning a curved seam in sewing. It is necessary to release the pressure upon the fabric (the paper, in this case).

You now have one-half of the piece perfectly in place. The other half is hanging free. Press that other half of the sheet against the adjoining wall. Start pressing in the middle of the sheet and not at the top or bottom. Smooth it out with your Applicator Smoother. As you are attaching the paper to the wall, be sure that it does not pull out from the corner. I find it helps if I hold the paper in the corner with my left hand while smoothing it with my right hand (or vice versa).

After you have pressed the middle third of the sheet against the wall, you will need your level. Run it vertically along the edge of the paper that is stuck to the wall. Be very sure that the bubbles are exactly centered. This is the only way you can be absolutely certain that the pattern will be perfectly straight around the entire room. Professional hangers usually don't bother to take the time to do this. If you don't take the time to check, you may find that when you hang that all-important last piece, its pattern does not exactly match the first piece you hung. So take the time and use the level. Make any corrections now, either by pushing the paper further into the corner or slightly moving it out.

Now press the top third of the paper against the wall and check it with the level. If it should be a little off, make a V-shaped cut starting at the ceiling and going down about one inch. Then butt the two cut edges together and no one will be the wiser (see Illustration 40).

If the top corner is slightly recessed, the paper will not reach into the corner and still be level on the adjoining wall. All that is needed here is to push a little spackle into the corner, smoothing it out so that the paper will fit tightly into the corner. No cutting is necessary.

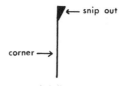

Illustration 40

Press the bottom third of the wallpaper sheet onto the wall. Make one last check with the level, guiding it all the way down the edge. Trim the excess paper off the ceiling and the baseboard, and your corner is turned. That really wasn't so difficult, was it?

An outside corner is turned in the same way except, instead of pressing the paper into the corner, you will be wrapping around an edge.

When you come to a light switch or outlet (remember, you have removed all the cover plates before beginning), take your scissors and make a rough cut in the paper around the opening. Be careful not to make too large a cut, or the cover plates will not hide the edges.

Cut just enough out so that the paper lies flat on the wall.

Prepasted paper is hung in the same manner as the unpasted kind, with one exception: it is not necessary to fold it into thirds. Cut the sheet to size (adding the necessary extra two inches) and roll it up starting with the bottom of the sheet. This leaves the top of the wallpaper sheet on the outside of the roll. Immerse the rolled-up piece in the water bucket. I have found that lukewarm water works much better on the paste than does cold. Leave the sheet in the water about thirty seconds. Turn it frequently so that the water can be absorbed into the inner circle. When removing the sheet from the water bucket, take the top edge with both hands. Pull it out slowly from the bucket as you mount the ladder. The slower you pull it, the surer you are that every section is thoroughly wet.

Match the pattern exactly as previously explained. Using a wet dishcloth or the Applicator Smoother, wipe the face of the paper, making quite sure that the entire sheet is thoroughly wet. Any small bubbles that appear can be removed with a pin. With prepasted paper it is necessary to wash the entire sheet thoroughly with clean water after it has been hung to remove the paste on the face of the paper due to the soaking in the water bucket. Also, change the water in the bucket frequently.

Many people are afraid to tackle hanging wallpaper on a wall next to a stairway. True, the sheet that extends from the ceiling on the second floor to the bottom of the first step may be sixteen feet, or more, in length. A basement stairway has a drop of approximately eight feet, although this figure can vary greatly.

Don't shy away from papering next to a stairway unless you are terrified of heights. The job usually requires the use of a scaffold (the plank of wood that painters use when painting a ceiling). If your stairway is an "open" one (for example, an L-shaped or U-shaped upstairs hallway), you can put one end of this plank across the top step and the other end on the second floor landing (see Illustration 40a).

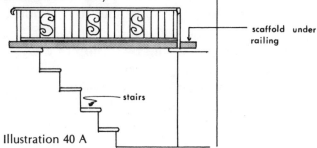

Illustration 40 A

Should you have a "closed" stairway, meaning that directly opposite the top stair (or landing) there is a solid wall, then you will need a ladder. The ladder must be tall enough so that the scaffold, when resting on the second to the top rung of the ladder, will be perfectly even with the second story landing (see Illustration 40b).

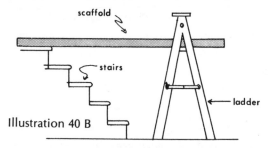

Illustration 40 B

Perhaps the last sheet of paper you hung before you came to the stairway is four or five inches away from the long wall next to the stairs. Some people advise cutting a "filler piece" for this space and using one continuous sheet down the long drop. Don't do it! The patchwork-quilt look will be obvious; the cut edge will show, the pattern may not match, and the end result will not be satisfying.

Finish papering the downstairs hall (in a two-story home) until you are within one width of the paper, or less, of the sheet that will go up the stairway area. Set up your scaffolding. Remember to assemble all the necessary tools first and keep them within reach—in wallpapering, this would be on top of the ladder.

Measure the length of the wallpaper drop, starting with the longest piece you will use. Since you will need to match the pattern on the adjoining sheet already in place, keep this in mind when cutting the long sheet. Measure the width of the wall between the last piece of wallpaper hung and the point where the long ceiling drop begins. You must also remember to allow for the one inch excess on the ceiling, on the floor or baseboard, and around any existing molding. *Don't cut too short.*

Although the scaffolding is set, do not start at the top. (This would not be true when papering a basement stairway, but would be true after wallpapering a foyer and having to continue up a stairway.) You must match the pattern on the adjoining sheet. Therefore, you will match and butt the paper to its mate starting at the top of the last piece hung. In the case of most stairways leading from a foyer, this will be eight feet from the floor. It does help if you have a partner to hold the top section of the wallpaper out of your way. However, my helper was afraid to walk on the scaffolding, so I temporarily stuck the top section onto the wall in one place so it wouldn't flop on my head.

Once you have matched, butted, and seam-rolled the lower portion, it's time to mount the scaffold. Keep your level with you. Walk across the scaffold and begin to smooth the upper portion of the wallpaper sheet into place. Most important, keep running that level along the outside edge of the paper (the side that has no paper next to it on the lower wall), making sure that the vertical level bubbles are centered. Should this piece not be hung perfectly straight, the rest of the wallpaper on the stairway will be slanted—the sign of an amateur!

With this piece in place, the rest of the stairwell is papered exactly as you did the straight wall. Keep in mind that if you chose a patterned paper, the pattern of each sheet must match the one on either side. Trimming off the excess inch on both the ceiling and the stairs is done exactly as outlined for wallpapering a straight wall.

Now that you have completed your papering, doesn't it look great? Maybe those old cover plates that go over the light switches and the outlets look shoddy in comparison with the "new" room. Why not visit your local discount store and purchase new ones? In most homes the cover plates are simple flat white ones. You'll be amazed at the variety that is now offered. There are colonial, modern, traditional, and novelty plates that will go with any decor. Perhaps you may even wish to cover the old plates with the new wallpaper.

Don't put the old ones back on until you have checked out the new ones available. The cost is nominal and they can make a big difference in the appearance of a room. Remember, you have already saved so much money by papering the room yourself that a few more dollars spent on outlet and switch covers may "make the room."

You're done! Stand back, take a bow, and be very, very proud.

Resilient Flooring

The name "resilient flooring" comes from the fact that the material used is pliable and fairly soft underfoot. Resilient flooring can usually be cut with a scissors or with a sharp razor (and a straightedge).

This type of flooring may be used in dens, kitchens, basements, family rooms, and, in some instances, bathrooms and entryways. It may be vinyl, vinyl asbestos, asphalt, rubber, cork, or linoleum. The choice is limited only by your imagination and the area in which you want to install the tile.

Some types of resilient flooring do not lend themselves to below-grade installation (for example, in a basement or a family room that is below the grass level of your home). Some are not suitable for installation on a cement slab. Many times a home that does not have a basement is built directly on cement that was poured on the ground. When purchasing tile, be sure to ask your dealer whether it is suitable for the place you wish to tile.

Most of us live in houses that were built a few years (or more) ago. At that time the choice in tile was small. One tile looked like the next, except for a slight difference in color and pattern. I painted my kitchen umpteen times, changed the decor in the den, and still looked at the same old floor tile. It is almost impossible to renovate a room and achieve a totally new look while keeping that "old floor."

Today you can get tile that looks like marble or slate (perhaps for your entry) or brick or stone (for a family room, den, or kitchen). Tiles come in imitation wood patterns that go well in any room where you want the ease of cleaning and the look of wood. You can also find imitation ceramic tile that you may want to use in an entryway or in a bathroom without having the extra expense of real ceramic tile.

Vinyl sheet flooring can be used indoors and out. If your kitchen or family room opens directly onto a patio via sliding glass doors, you might wish to carry the floor pattern to the outside.

So before you choose a new floor covering, look at many samples. You will truly be amazed at the wide variety of patterns and materials available to you. But be sure to tell your tile dealer in which room you plan to install the new floor. Then he will be able to show you samples of the correct type of tile to use in your particular situation.

When you enter the tile store to make your selection, you will be stunned at the difference in price for what, to you, look like comparable materials. There is even a wide price range in vinyl asbestos floor coverings. Maybe the following pointers will help clear up a confusing situation.

Resilient floor tiles can be purchased in many different sizes. There are tiles that are nine inches square and twelve inches square, and some that are as large as eighteen inches. Needless to say, the larger the tile, the more the cost. But you also need to consider that you would only need one-fourth as many eighteen-inch squares as you would nine-inch squares to complete the same room, so the cost difference might not actually be that great in the long run. Also, the larger the tile, the less time it will take you to finish the floor. And there will be fewer seams to detract from the overall uniform look.

Cork tile is probably the most expensive flooring that an amateur would attempt to put down. However, I don't recommend it for the average home with children and pets. True, it is luxurious looking and quiet underfoot, but it does take special care. A sealer must be applied to it periodically or dirt and grit get ground in. If cork appeals to you, try the imitation type. To most people it looks as good as the real thing, but it requires none of the upkeep.

Rubber tile is rarely seen in the stores anymore. It has a tendency to be dented by furniture and to scuff easily. It also does not hold the shine that so many homemakers consider a necessity.

Plain asphalt tile is the cheapest of all tiles, but it is difficult to maintain. Grease and oil will seep into its surface and permanently mar it, and it will not hold a wax shine. But most important to the do-it-yourselfer is the fact that asphalt tile has a tendency to chip and crack when it is cut.

Linoleum is sold in sheets anywhere from six feet to twelve feet in width. It is not difficult to put down, but it, too, does not hold a shine as well as some of the newer types of flooring.

Sheet goods (materials that come in a long roll and must be cut to size) are also available in solid vinyl or vinyl asbestos. These have a permanent wax finish built into them and need little, or no, upkeep.

Vinyl asbestos tile is far and away the best seller today. This type of tile is called "vinyl asbestos" because a vinyl top layer has been adhered to a more substantial asbestos base. This makes a very strong tile. It is easy to lay and is stronger than solid vinyl as far as denting is concerned, and it can be used anywhere in the home from the basement to the attic. An added bonus is that the newest tiles have a permanent shine built right into them. Just damp mop, and your floor will look as though you spent all day waxing it. Vinyl asbestos is a little more expensive than plain asbestos, but I think it is worth the added cost because it saves you time and energy.

Even with vinyl or vinyl asbestos, you will find a wide range of prices. This is due to the difference in the thickness of the vinyl. Solid vinyl costs more than vinyl asbestos because the vinyl asbestos has only a veneer (topping) of vinyl on top of cheaper material. However, solid vinyl is so soft that it dents easily and is prone to show up any irregularity in the floor beneath it.

Vinyl and vinyl asbestos come in one-sixteenth inch, one-eighth inch, and one-fourth inch thicknesses. The thickness is called the gauge of the tile. The heavier the gauge, the more expensive the tile. However, I think you will find that thicker tiles hold up longer.

There is one other type of resilient flooring that you may wish to consider. It will cost more than ordinary vinyl, but you will save money because you will not need mastic (and mastic is not cheap!). Labor, too, is diminished because you don't need to spread the glue. This is the "peel and stick" tile. This type of tile is usually vinyl asbestos, and some brands have the built-in shine feature that appeals to homemakers.

The principle is simple. There is a tacky substance (much like the sticky stuff on Scotch tape) on the back of each tile. The back is covered with a piece of wax paper. You simply pull off the paper and lay the tile in place. When cutting a piece of tile to fit the edge of a room, you leave the paper on until you are quite sure that the piece will fit correctly. Then you remove the paper and lay the tile on the floor.

Let me mention one fact about self-stick tile which I learned the hard way. No matter what the manufacturer claims, self-stick tiles have a tendency to move on the floor, especially in heavy traffic areas. This is to be expected because the adhesive is not as strong as mastic. I don't mean to knock "peel and stick" tile. I've used it myself. If you choose this tile, make the edge pieces fit tightly to the baseboard. This may help prevent the rest of the tiles from moving.

One very important point to remember when using self-stick tiles: keep a large garbage bag handy and immediately throw away the backing paper as you remove it. Because the paper has a wax coating, it is extremely slippery. Step on one of those papers, slip, and the hospital bills will wipe out any savings you would have realized by doing it yourself.

I have a friend who, while putting down self-stick tile, kept warning her children to stay away from the discarded papers. The children obeyed, but you can guess what happened. She stepped back to view her work, slipped on a backing sheet, and wound up in bed for a week with sprains and bruises. So keep that garbage bag handy and throw away each piece of paper as you peel it off.

If you do not use self-stick tile, you will need to buy mastic. Be sure to purchase the mastic at the same time you buy the tile. The dealer will sell you the correct type of mastic for the tile you have picked. It is vitally important that you have the correct kind for your tile. Be very sure to tell the supplier where you intend to lay the tile. There are different types of mastic for different surfaces. So tell your dealer whether you plan to lay a tile floor over cement in the basement or over an existing floor in a kitchen or den.

Before you lay your new floor, bring the cartons of tile into the room that you intend to work in and open them up. Let the tiles sit in the room for at least forty-eight hours so that they will be accustomed to the humidity. This may sound a little crazy, but tiles contract or expand according to the weather and the conditions in your house. Tile that is left in a cold garage until you use it will have a tendency to expand on the floor, and this could cause buckling. Conversely, tile that has been warm and then is laid on a cold basement cement floor may shrink, causing the seams to be very noticeable.

An earlier chapter covered the basic steps in laying a ceramic tile floor. The same steps are followed when laying a resilient tile floor.

It is possible to lay a new floor over an existing one if you have properly prepared the old floor. If the existing floor is of embossed tile (meaning that it has definite up-and-down pattern indentations on it), then the new tile will not lie smoothly. It will be necessary either to remove the tile or to lay a quarter-inch underlayment before tiling. Since the underlayment would raise the floor level, plus cost much more in labor and money, I suggest removing the existing tile and sanding the floor smooth.

This procedure is the same as outlined in the chapter on preparing to lay ceramic tile. You must have a clean floor, and it must be free of dents, cuts, chips, or lumps. With ceramic tile you can afford not to fill in every little dent because the mastic is applied heavily and the tile itself is so thick. However, vinyl (and I'll use this term to cover all resilient flooring) is flexible and thin. Any imperfection in the original flooring beneath it will show through. So take extra care in the proper preparation of the old floor and you will be rewarded with a perfectly smooth new floor.

You cannot lay vinyl tile over ceramic tile because it will not adhere properly. Ceramic tile must be removed as described in Chapter 2 and the underflooring prepared accordingly.

Start by removing the quarter round or base shoe, if they are present, as outlined in Chapter 2. Do this before cleaning the floor because there will be a dirt build-up where the quarter round meets the floor. You may have to scrape up this dirt with a knife, but make very sure that it is all removed.

I'll not go into much detail about the actual laying of a vinyl tile floor, as it is installed in essentially the same way as was described in the chapter on laying ceramic floor tile. However, there is one important difference. You must be sure that any dents or holes are filled in with spackle and sanded smooth. If any of the old tiles are loose, then cement them in place first, because the new tile will stay on the floor only as long as the original does. So get down on your knees and *inspect* the old floor closely! Fill in all the holes, sand down the lumps, and cement any loose tiles in place.

Now clean the old floor thoroughly. Use a wax-stripper and an electric scrubber. Soap and rinse until the rinse water is perfectly clear. You must remove all wax and dirt if you want the new floor to adhere properly. Allow it to dry thoroughly.

It would be very easy to lay the new tiles directly on top of the old without bothering to find the center line of the area to be tiled. I cannot emphasize too strongly that you should *not* do this. If tile is going to pull loose, it will do so at the seams. To lay one tile directly over another (existing) tile is asking for trouble. If the bottom tile pulls loose, the top tile is going to come right up with it.

Should you be laying tile squares over sheet goods, again, do not have one tile edge directly in line with the original seam. If water seeps between the tiles, the bottom layer will not dry out, and your entire new floor could come loose.

Remember to keep your vacuum cleaner right next to you and vacuum just before you lay each tile. This will eliminate dust or dirt particles that would show through the new tile as unsightly lumps.

In the chapter on ceramic tile, I described how to determine the center of a room and the starting point in laying tile. The same directions should be followed when laying vinyl tile. Try to keep the end tiles as even in width as possible, corresponding with the opposite side of the wall.

If the existing tile on the floor is perfectly centered, both in width and length, it is possible to use these lines to find the starting point. Remember, however, do not lay the edge of the new tile directly on the old seam line. Take your ruler and measure out from the center seam line about one inch. Make your marks all the way down the vertical center line of the room, and then, using **a** yardstick or a ruler, connect these marks. Repeat the same procedure on the horizontal center line (see Illustration 41).

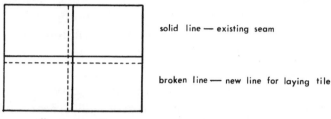

solid line — existing seam

broken line — new line for laying tile

Illustration 41

Now you have established your starting point without all the bother of measuring from one end of the room to the other, both vertically and horizontally. You may have cheated a little, but you've saved yourself considerable time and you will have eliminated any chance of having seams in the new floor fall directly on top of an existing seam.

I have found that most vinyl tiles cut easily with a sharp scissors. You may have a blister or two on your thumb, but if you've ever cut folded corduroy, you've probably experienced blisters in the same place.

If you chose asphalt tile, you will find it has a tendency to chip. I have found a solution to this problem but I don't know if the manufacturer would recommend it. Almost every oven has a low heat cycle (125° or less). Turn your oven on to this low heat, lay the tile in it for about forty-five seconds, and you will find that it cuts like silk. Cut it to size while it is still soft, but wait until it hardens before you lay it in the mastic. Remember, tile expands under heat and will shrink when cooled. By using your oven, you can cut six or seven edge pieces in succession. While the first one is returning to room temperature, you can cut the remaining pieces. Not only have you saved time, but you've saved your thumb! This procedure can also be used on vinyl asbestos tile.

The laying of vinyl tile differs in one important way from the laying of ceramic tile. In laying ceramic tile you can apply a little more mastic than is absolutely necessary. Ceramic is thick enough that a slight excess of mastic will not show. Vinyl tile is thinner. Mastic will ooze up between the tiles, making for a messy job. But, far more important, too much mastic will prevent the tiles from butting tightly together. No matter what the size of the tile, you want the floor to look like one continuous piece when it is completed.

The use of too much mastic is a mark of an amateur. So use it sparingly, and use the small-toothed side of the spreader—unless the mastic directions distinctly say to use the larger teeth. Never, never spread mastic beyond the point where you are going to lay your last tile before quitting time. Far better to be short on mastic than to apply too much. It will spread when you exert the pressure necessary to adhere the tile. Do not finish one box of tile before opening the next box. Better to mix them up a little. There can be a difference in the tiles even though the run is the same.

Some tiles have arrows stamped on the back showing the vertical line of the pattern. If a tile must match the pattern of the tile directly next to it (as in a pebble or stone pattern), then the arrows should all point in one direction. If there is no match from tile to tile, you should alternate the direction of the arrows (see Illustration 42). Then, if there is some slight difference in the color or texture of the tiles, it will not be so noticeable. The directions that come with each box of tile will probably suggest which way to place the arrows.

When you lay tile on mastic, it is imperative that you

do not push the tile into place. To do so would move the mastic, which would come up between the tiles, thereby

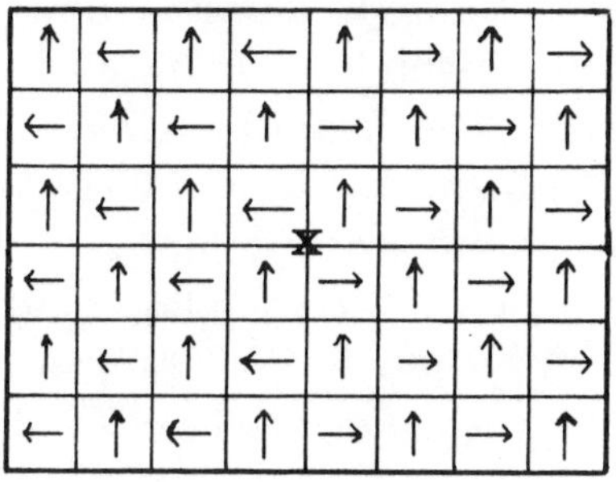

↑	←	↑	←	↑	→	↑	→
←	↑	←	↑	→	↑	→	↑
↑	←	↑	←	↑	→	↑	→
←	↑	←	↑	→	↑	→	↑
↑	←	↑	←	↑	→	↑	→
←	↑	←	↑	→	↑	→	↑

'x' is center line

Illustration 42

causing them to not fit snugly together. Instead, take a tile, lay it barely over the one next to it, and snap it into place. This way, the slight push you give it will be away from the seam. However, be sure that you fit the tiles tightly together.

When you are cutting the edge pieces, it is easy to forget that the manufacturer's finished edge must be the one that will abut against another tile. The edge you cut, the one that will not be perfectly straight, is the one that must go next to the wall. There really is no trick to measuring these pieces. Just turn the piece to be cut over on its face (so you are looking at the back side). Fit it up to the wall with part of it overlapping the last tile set in place. Draw a line across the back of the tile where it meets the other tile. Cut along this line. Turn the cut tile over, reverse it so that its finished edge meets the finished edge of the adjoining tile, and set it in place.

One last hint on laying square tiles. Use your feet to push them tightly into place (do this after you have snapped them into the mastic). Lean on the wall or against the kitchen counter and exert pressure on the tile. Then you will be assured of a tight fit.

Sheet goods are a little trickier to lay. Sheet goods come in six-foot, nine-foot, and twelve-foot widths. I don't recommend that a woman try to lay a twelve-foot-wide piece herself. Even a nine-foot sheet is unwieldy to handle, but you can work with it if you have patience.

Sheet goods are not laid from the center of the room as you do with tiles. Instead, start from the longest wall you have and measure out from it the width of the goods. Make four or five marks on the floor and, using your ruler, join them together. This will be your guideline for the first sheet. The other pieces will follow the preceding sheet. Be sure to follow the manufacturer's directions closely when laying sheet goods or they will come apart at the seams.

Sheet goods must be cut to size before installation. A sharp razor blade held in a handle will cut most tile, though some may be cut with scissors. Measure the length you need, and cut it. It needn't fit perfectly to the wall. The quarter round will cover any small gap. Roll the piece up and spread the mastic on a portion of the floor (for example, the width of the piece by three feet in length). Press this section into place. Then spread more mastic and unroll more of the sheet, setting it into place. Continue until the sheet is laid.

Put the quarter round back on the baseboard as previously explained and you are done! You can walk on the floor, but don't wash it for three or four days. Give the mastic time to thoroughly dry. Wait two days or so before moving heavy furniture onto the new floor. Granted, it is nice to see the room completed, but don't take a chance on marring your new floor. Heavy furniture can also press the mastic out.

Doesn't the room look great? And, again, you did it all yourself!

5
The Kitchen

There are so many things that you can do to improve a kitchen without a great outlay of money that I hardly know where to begin. We women spend a great deal of our time in the kitchen. We're either making meals, cleaning up after them, or just sitting at the kitchen table visiting with a neighbor. When your friends pop in for an impromptu visit, what room do you gravitate to? Probably not the living room or even the den—after all, where is the coffee pot? In the kitchen.

Most of us hate to get up in the morning, and to go into a depressing kitchen makes it that much harder. So, let's do something about that room without spending too much money.

Look around your kitchen. Is it dingy looking? All too often we only repaint the walls and change the curtains. But the end result is usually less than satisfying. New paint or wallpaper may make the cabinets and the floor look that much worse. A perfect example is my own kitchen. The floor and the counter top were off-white. First I painted the walls aqua. The second time around it was yellow. Three years later I decided I'd like a pink kitchen. By this time, the off-white floor looked more like dirty grey. It ruined the entire room. So I chose lime-green floor tile, installed it, and the room took on a totally new atmosphere—cheerful and, best of all, new.

Since you already know how to lay a floor, there's no need to go into that again. But perhaps you would like to carpet your kitchen. Kitchen carpet is sold either in squares or by the roll. Make sure that you purchase carpeting made for kitchen use—such as an indoor-outdoor type that is treated to resist stains.

Carpet squares usually have an adhesive already applied, and are laid in exactly the same manner as "peel and stick" resilient tile. Kitchen carpet sold in rolls is installed with strips of sticky tape. If you decide on carpeting, look at the beautiful patterns that are available. A pattern hides the seams (and the dirt).

Not many of us can afford to install new cabinets in the kitchen. The cost is high and installation requires a great deal of labor. I do not recommend that a woman attempt to install cabinets. They are heavy, and a pretty good knowledge of carpentry is necessary to install them properly. However, there is a line of prefinished cabinets, each a complete unit in itself, with doors already attached. The units are packed individually. Although I have never hung one of these units, the directions are simple, and the installation does not appear to be difficult.

If you choose to remove the old cabinets and install new ones, one word of warning. Should you have a built-in oven or range, do not attempt to install the cabinets that contain these units by yourself. Removing an oven or range, whether it be gas or electric, is no job for the amateur. The risk of fire or explosion is too great. This is one time to call in a professional.

But if you don't wish to replace the cabinets, why not just revamp them? Most of the cabinets installed years ago were made of "blond" wood. Today, that isn't "in." So why not darken them to walnut or dark oak? Or antique them?

Consider dark red or green, if that appeals to you. A white background with gold flecks in it lends itself very well to provincial decor. If you use an antiquing kit, the job is easy. Go to a large paint store or a building-supplies dealer and see the great variety of kits from which you can choose. Remember to scrub the cabinets down with a good detergent to remove dirt, grease, and wax before painting them. Also, remove the handles for a much easier (and neater) job.

Don't discount the use of Con-Tact paper on cabinets. There are many beautiful patterns available—floral patterns, stripes, and imitations of wood. If you have thoroughly cleaned the face of the cabinets before applying the paper, you will have no trouble with its pulling loose. Should a piece rip sometime in the future, you can easily replace it, so always buy a little more than you need for the job.

Today's cabinets usually are decorated with extruded moldings. These are easy to apply. Decorative moldings come in many shapes and sizes. An example would be a square molding that lends itself to traditional decor (see Illustration 43). Your lumber dealer can show you samples. Moldings can be nailed to the existing wood cabinets or glued on (using interior glue). My preference is gluing; then there are no nail holes that must then be filled in with putty before staining. Filled-in holes are often discernible after painting or "touching up."

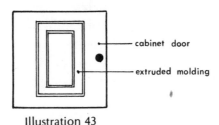

cabinet door

extruded molding

Illustration 43

If you have chosen to apply extruded moldings, paint or stain them before applying them to the cabinet doors. To do so afterward will cause a paint buildup around the edges. If you are antiquing the cabinets, putting the moldings on before painting will prevent you from making the straight lines on the finish coat that make for the authentic antique look. So finish your cabinets first, and then the moldings. When both have dried, glue the molding to the doors.

Remove all the handles from your cabinets before painting. You may find that you want new hardware. It is not inexpensive, but when you compare the cost of hardware with that of totally new cabinets, the amount spent is not great. If you do choose to purchase new handles, be sure that the screw holes fit the existing holes in the cabinets. The easiest way to do this is to remove an old handle and take it to the store when purchasing the new ones. Then you will know that the new handles will have the same space between the screw holes as the old handles.

Maybe you wish to use the old hardware, but it looks a little seedy. Get a can of spray paint—copper, silver, gold, or whatever you wish. Take the handles outside (spray paint makes a mess for miles around), lay them on newspaper, and spray away. You probably won't recognize them as the same old hardware you removed. I would recommend using a paint made especially for metal; otherwise the paint will peel or chip. Shellac the handles to protect them.

Make sure you clean the handles thoroughly before painting, as kitchen grease will prevent any paint from adhering. Any good household cleaner will remove the dirt and grease.

You can sand your cabinets down to the bare wood and varnish them for a natural finish. The most important factor to remember is that you must make your kitchen an extension of your own personality.

Above the cabinets in some kitchens is an area that is roughly thirteen inches in length which extends down from the ceiling to meet the cabinet edge. This is called the soffit. It may also be above the oven and the stove, where most of the grease is deposited on the walls. You can make the soffit the focal point of the room by using washable Con-Tact or wallpaper.

A few years ago I bought Con-Tact paper with a shiny vinyl finish. It has large flowers of pink, yellow, and green, with black stems. I had some afterthoughts about its peeling off the walls, but these were totally unfounded. The Con-Tact paper is still there, washes beautifully, and adds to the decor of the kitchen. I also cut out some of the flowers and applied them to the walls of the breakfast area.

If you choose a wallpaper rather than Con-Tact, be sure that it is both washable and scrubbable. This is vitally important in a kitchen. You certainly don't want to go to the expense and work of hanging paper and then find out that when you wash it, it either fades or peels. Wallpaper is sold in soffit lengths; this is commonly called trim paper. It comes in a great variety of patterns and colors, so be sure to ask for it when looking at the wallpaper books.

Another idea for redoing your kitchen is to use paneling on the walls rather than paint or wallpaper. All too often we tend to think of a paneled kitchen as Early American or rustic. This is not necessarily true. The paneling offered today can be as old fashioned or as modern as you wish. Although wood paneling used to come only in traditional wood tones, today it is available in a variety of colors. Some is finished with a vinyl coating that resists grease and dirt and is easy to keep clean. I suggest that you pick one that is smooth to the touch. A rough surface would be difficult to clean thoroughly because grease would accumulate in the recesses. Also, use hardboard paneling rather than solid wood, as wood cannot be easily cleaned of kitchen grease.

Another thought would be to use MarLite panels. They come in many different colors, patterns, and textures. They are easy to keep clean and to install (much like paneling, but follow the manufacturer's instructions). The panels go up quickly and easily with simple clips (should you choose the plank style) or adhesive. Moldings that match, or contrast with, the panels are also available. However, keep one fact in mind. The panels do scratch, regardless of the promises made. Therefore, you may not wish to use them in an area where they could easily be marred.

Regardless of the type you choose, paneling will be much more expensive than paint, and also more work. So use great care before deciding upon a certain material and color or pattern.

A kitchen counter top can be an eyesore. Perhaps it has been scratched by improperly used knives (Formica is not impervious to cuts, although many people think differently) or is peeling due to age. Or maybe you just don't like it.

I do not suggest that you install an entire new counter top (meaning not just the surface but the whole piece that tops the wood base). Installing an entire new top requires expertise. It is no job for an amateur or even a do-it-yourselfer who thinks she knows what she's doing.

There is one product that I will give short mention to in case you are considering changing your counter top. The product is a tough, flexible plastic covering that comes in patterns and textures that imitate slate, stone, leather, and other materials. You can use it on a counter, a bar, or a table. The color goes all the way through, so it can't rub off. It resists spills, food stains, scuffing, and common household chemicals. I am not going to describe its installation since you can contact a dealer in your area. Full instructions are given with any order.

Another solution to that counter top that you totally dislike is ceramic tile. If you have a large counter top you can use the large tiles. But most kitchens lend themselves better to the one-inch-square tiles, commonly called mosaic, or the random pebble design. The variety available is almost endless.

Ceramic tile on a counter top is impressive. But, more important, it is virtually waterproof and cut proof. One company sells pregrouted sheets that need to be sealed only along edges at the wall and around fixtures. I have not used this product myself, so cannot recommend it by experience. The idea behind it is certainly time saving. However, this product will probably be more expensive than tile that you grout yourself.

If the existing Formica top on your counter is loose,

it must be glued down thoroughly before laying ceramic tiles. I suggest removing the Formica before setting ceramic. Formica has a shiny finish, and mastic may not stick to it. Should the original top come loose, the tile will pop up. Also, consider the edge tiles. They are the most prone to loosen; unless they are securely bonded, they will fall off.

One other point to consider—when you install ceramic tile you raise the counter height. If you install tile on top of an existing counter top, you will only raise the counter height that much more. Raising your sink and counter-top stove, if you have one, needn't present much difficulty, but the least amount you have to raise these heavy items, the better.

Taking off a Formica top is not difficult. It is much like removing tile from a floor. Start at one edge with a paint scraper or putty knife. Using a hammer, force the knife under the Formica. Raise it up and begin to peel it off. Using the knife as needed, you should be able to pull the entire sheet off the counter. The same technique is used on the backsplash (the piece that runs roughly four inches up the wall). The edging of the counter will come off easily when the top is removed.

Around your sink is a piece of stainless steel or aluminum that covers the opening where the sink meets the counter. This may also be present around a built-in stove top. In order to install ceramic tile, it is necessary to raise this piece so it will cover the tile. Under the sink are screws that hold it in place. These must be loosened so you can lay the tile under the metal strip. Be very careful! A double sink weighs approximately eighty-five pounds. You could be seriously injured were it to drop on you while you are loosening the screws. This is not a bad time to ask for help. If you are doing it yourself, loosen the screws only enough to slightly release the rim. Be sure the sink itself is still firmly on the screws.

After you have removed all the Formica, you probably will have to sand down the mastic that is left on the plywood base. Normally a hand sander or just sandpaper and a lot of sweat will do the job. From the chapter on laying ceramic floor tile, you will recall that you can afford to have a few small lumps of mastic left. The new mastic and the thickness of the tile will hide any small imperfections.

Ceramic tile, one inch square (sometimes referred to as mosaic tile when used on counter tops or tables), is sold in sheets. Lay a few of these sheets out on the counter. Move them around so that you will have the least amount of cutting along the edges.

The most important step to consider when looking for a starting point is this: the tile must extend past the edge of the counter to the extent of the thickness of the tile. Otherwise, when you tile the side edge, it will stand out from the top. The top tiles must cover the side pieces for a professional-looking job. I don't want to make this sound complicated as it really isn't. If the tile is three-eighths of an inch thick, the tile on the counter top should extend three-eighths of an inch beyond the edge. This way the finished edge will be on the surface and not on the side. (You may prefer using "cap tile" around the edges, which is explained later.)

When you have arranged a few tile sheets so that there will be a minimum number of cuts, draw a line on the counter top with a pen to show where you are going to place the first sheet. Spread the mastic and lay the tile. Check to see that it is straight, using the carpenter's square and a ruler. Continue laying the tile, just as you did on the floor.

The sink has been loosened. Lay the tile up to the edge of the sink hole and underneath the steel strip. This area should now be grouted since you want to reattach the sink as soon as possible. It does entail a little more work to mix some grout before you are ready to grout the entire surface. But it is important to tighten those sink screws immediately. You don't want that sink to drop!

The same principle holds true if you have a counter-top stove. You must loosen the stove to lay the ceramic tile under it. Otherwise you will not have an even counter surface. Loosen the stove screws, set your tile, grout it, and tighten the screws. They are loosened and tightened from underneath the stove. Very easy to do!

After the entire counter is finished, it is time to tile the backsplash. The backsplash is the four-inch section that meets the back edge of the counter and extends up the wall. If you have removed the Formica, there is a plywood backing still in place. This must be covered with tile. You will begin with the top of the backsplash, just as you did with the top of the counter. Normally, this area is three-fourths of an inch wide. Measure it to make sure. You must remember, as you did with the counter top, that the top piece must extend over the edge the thickness of the tile. The finished edge must always be on top. It's not a bad idea to purchase cap tile for this edge and also for the counter-top edges. Cap tile has a rounded edge that gives a finished look to the job. As cap tile is more expensive than regular tile, don't buy too many more tiles than you need. In other words, measure!

Should the top (or cap) tile be too large (that is, if it extends beyond the top of the backsplash plus the thickness of one tile), make any necessary cuts on the edge that will butt up against the wall. The jagged edges of these cuts are easily filled in with the grout and will not show.

The front of the backsplash is usually four inches in height. Don't try to set each piece of tile individually. Take a full sheet of tile and cut it to fit the vertical space (see Illustration 44). You should not have to cut any of the tiles, since most backsplashes are divisible by one inch. Should you have to cut any, do so where the tile meets the top of the backsplash. Since none of us is three feet tall, who's to notice if there is some slight imperfection? That's what grout is for!

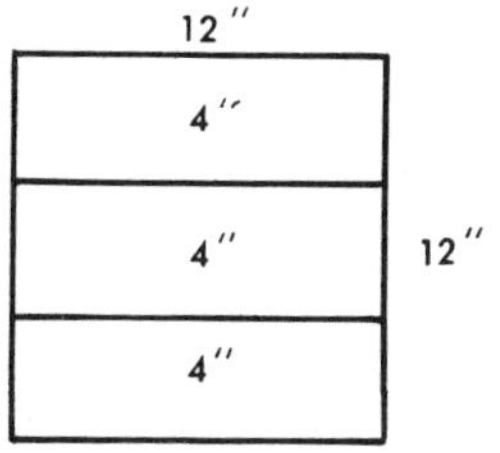

Illustration 44

If your counter is curved or oval in shape on one end, it will be necessary to cut the top tile to fit (unless you have used a random pebble pattern tile and you are able to remove individual tiles and set them in according to size).

The cutting is done with tile snippers. Take very small snips, remembering to leave the overhang. It does take a lot of time and patience, but the final result is worth it. By cutting only a little bit off at one time you will reduce the chance of having the entire tile shatter. Normally, the edge tiles will not need to be cut. Although they do not bend, you can fit them around a curve by using more, or less, mastic. Let your fingers be your guide.

The only thing left to do is the grouting, which is

done exactly as outlined in the chapter on ceramic tiling a floor.

It's possible that your counter is in perfect condition, and you don't wish to replace it. Perhaps only the wall area above it (and below the cabinets) looks shoddy. The area above the stove and around the sink takes the worst beating. Food and water are constantly splashing on these walls. You wash them much more than you do the rest of the kitchen. They fade and look the worse for wear, while the rest of the kitchen may be in perfect condition.

You are probably saying to yourself, "She's going to recommend ceramic tile." You're right, but only partly. Yes, I do recommend ceramic tile. It is easy to keep clean and it always keeps its sheen. Even the grout is easy to clean with one of the bathroom tile cleaners. In the chapter on remodeling a bathroom I will cover tiling walls.

You can also use Con-Tact paper or scrubbable wallpaper in this section. Nothing wrong with them—they are beautiful if they are matched to your decor.

Now for a different idea for this area. Copper and stainless steel tiles are made in approximately four-inch squares. They are impressive looking and easy to install. Most come with adhesive already applied—just like "peel and stick" floor tile.

However, no matter how beautiful, they are, they do have their drawbacks. They spot easily and need a special metal cleaner to make them shine. But, far and away, their greatest fault is that they dent easily. After all, if you throw a pan at your husband and miss, you don't need a dented wall as a constant reminder. Yet, if you are even-tempered and don't mind the extra work of keeping them shiny, metal tiles are, to me, the most beautiful tiles you can use in the kitchen work area.

Metal tiles are put in place like other types of tile. However, you must be careful not to press them too hard in the center. They will buckle. If you have not chosen the "peel and stick" kind, you will need a special adhesive. Be sure to purchase this when you buy the tiles.

It is highly unlikely that the area to be tiled will be exactly divisible by the four-inch tiles. Therefore, start at the edge where the backsplash meets the wall and work upward. If tiles must be cut, cut the ones that will butt up against the cabinet bottom so that the cuts won't be so noticeable.

It is extremely hard to make a perfect cut in copper and stainless steel tiles because of their pliability. Some tile men will tell you to cut them with a saber saw; others will say to use tin snips. (Tin snips look like the tool you use when pruning roses. If you don't have roses, then they resemble a pair of large pliers with sharp edges.) Ask your dealer what he recommends, and then if it doesn't work you can always go back to him and complain. I used tin snips and found they worked perfectly. But that was many years ago; perhaps there are even better methods now. This is another reason why I keep stressing that you must do business with a reputable dealer. He can be a great help.

Having now contemplated the walls, cabinets, floor, and counter top, it is time to look at the ceiling. Look at the ceiling? you say. What is there to see up there except paint? Mentioning paint brings up another thought. If you are going to paint your kitchen, whether it be the walls or the ceiling, be sure to use a semigloss enamel paint. It resists dirt and grime, and, far more important, it is a cinch to keep clean. Semigloss washes like a dream and will retain its color for years.

Rather than painting the ceiling, consider using ceiling tiles. I am not going to go into great detail here about ceiling tile because an entire chapter will deal with it later. So here are just a few pointers in case you are considering its use in the kitchen.

I would not say it is necessary to have acoustical tile in the kitchen. Usually a lot of noise does not emanate from a kitchen—unless you have noisy children! If I were tiling a kitchen ceiling, I would be more concerned with its scrubbability. It also stands to reason that tiles with a deeply cut pattern will be much more difficult to clean than smooth ones. One company produces tiles that are vinyl coated. I have not checked into the exact cost, but I do know they are more expensive than the regular tiles. In a kitchen, the extra cost would be worth it because of the accumulation of smoke and grease.

If you wish to use ceiling tile in the kitchen, follow the recommendations and instructions in the chapter on installing ceiling tile.

There may well be one annoying group of items in your kitchen that you cannot afford to replace—your large appliances. They probably work well, or you would replace them. So, either you don't like their color or they have become chipped and discolored over the years. To make them new looking is a simple job.

Have you seen the new paints that are made especially for kitchen appliances? You can paint a white refrigerator copper, yellow, avocado, or pink in no time at all. A colored appliance can be painted a new color, although I would not try covering a factory copper or stainless finish with porcelain paint. My opinion is that the paint would not adhere, but that is only an opinion, and perhaps I'm wrong.

These paints are sold in spray cans. True, it is more expensive to buy any paint in a spray can, but in the case of appliances, spray cans are the easiest thing to use. If you follow the instructions on the can, you will find that spray paints go on very smoothly and closely resemble a factory finish. To paint with a brush is asking for trouble. You will end up with uneven strokes and brush marks. Invest in a few cans of spray paint, and you will have a professional-looking job.

Before painting your refrigerator and stove, be sure to remove the handles. If it is not possible to remove them, cover or wrap them completely with masking tape. If you are painting a gas stove that you cannot remove from the kitchen, be sure all the pilot lights are out and the gas is turned off.

You will encounter one problem with painting appliances—moving them. If you live in a house, I suggest you move them outside. Spray paint is great, but it does spray over everything in sight. Once I spray-painted chairs for our poolroom. Rather than carry them upstairs, I did it in the basement. It took a professional cleaning man to remove the droplets of paint from the floor and walls. And I had covered everything within reach (I thought) with drop cloths and newspapers.

Although this is a book for women, the moving of appliances may not be a job for women. If you can't impose on a willing male (husband, neighbor, or whatever) to take the refrigerator outside, then it would certainly pay to have a handyman or a local teen-ager do it. I've never met a teen-age boy yet who wouldn't like to make a few extra bucks for a half-hour's work—taking the appliance out of your home and back in when you are done.

Of course, this is almost impossible if you live on the second or third floor of an apartment building. Then you will need a lot of newspaper. Cover the *entire* floor of your kitchen. Using Scotch tape or masking tape, fasten newspaper to the entire wall behind the appliance you intend to spray and any other wall near it. Remove all furniture from the room, and cover anything you can't move. Spray paint does stray!

If your water faucet is corroded or cheap looking, you may wish to replace it. One manufacturer puts out a do-it-yourself faucet. With ordinary tools you can install it in no time at all. Since the directions are clear and complete, I'm not going to repeat them. Suffice it to say that it is easy to do. Take a look when you are in your local hardware store, and decide if you want to attempt the installation.

See how easy it is to remodel your kitchen? An outlay of a few dollars combined with your time, talents, ideas, and energy and you have created a room fit for a queen—you!

The Bathroom

All too often people feel that changing the bathroom decor means changing the shower curtain, window curtains, towels, or rug. They make the assumption that the sink, toilet bowl, and walls are there to stay. This is not true, although to change the fixtures does entail expense.

Douglas Tuomey of the *Chicago Tribune* said: "A good look at a bathroom will reveal the true age of a house. This is one room where carpeting, paint, and wallpaper can't cover up old age. Just looking at the lavatory, tub, and lighting fixtures will help you date the age of a house within five years."

He continued: "One of the dead giveaways is the shower curtain hanging on a rod above the tub. No matter how new a house is, the shower curtain seems to make it appear older than it really is. Conversely, the bathroom in an older home can be made to look almost modern with the addition of a shower-tub enclosure."

I couldn't agree with Mr. Tuomey more. Not only are shower curtains outdated, but the plastic ones are difficult to wash without crinkling. The new satin-finished ones also must be washed with care. Not that a glass or plastic tub enclosure keeps itself clean. But you clean a tub enclosure as you do a window. Hard-water spots come off with an ammonia solution. Best of all, you don't have to take the enclosure off and put it back on as you do a shower curtain. Plus you remove the possibility of water leaking onto the floor when someone forgets to put the curtain inside the tub while taking a shower.

Installing a tub enclosure is really not difficult. There are two types. One is made of plastic. The other is con-structed of glass and usually comes in two sections. A glass enclosure has one big drawback if you have young children whom you must bathe. You have access to only one-half of the tub at a time. The sections slide, true, and will move either way. Regardless of how you slide them, however, one-half of the tub is closed. I think this makes it very difficult to bathe a one- or two-year-old child, who always seems to end up at the wrong end of the tub.

I think you'll agree that glass is beautiful. It can be clear, patterned, or frosted. Clear glass makes the room look larger, but it also shows soap and hard-water spots. Frosted glass does a better job of covering up for a lax housekeeper. Also, it hides the person taking a shower should someone else need to use the bathroom.

If you decide upon glass shower doors, be very, very sure that they are made of tempered glass. This is the term commonly used for glass that is break resistant. It is the same type that is used in windshields on cars. It may shatter into minute pieces if enough force is exerted upon it, but it will not break as a water glass does when dropped. Tempered glass costs more than ordinary glass, but you will never make a better investment in your life. And I do mean "your life." The emergency room staff of any hospital can tell you many stories of children (and adults) who have slipped in the tub or on the bathroom floor and fallen through ordinary-glass shower doors. Some have lived; some have not.

Although this is a chapter on bathrooms, the above paragraph has implications for other situations and merits a little more attention. Too often the sliding glass patio doors that are common today are not made of tempered glass. I have a good friend who keeps her house immaculate. Her husband added a room to their home but left the existing patio doors between the new room and the dining room. Rushing to go to Midnight Mass one Christmas Eve, she went through the door, literally, and almost died from loss of blood before the ambulance arrived. The physical and mental anguish could never be counted in dollars.

If you have sliding glass doors anywhere in your home that are not of tempered glass, put a few decorative decals on them. Then you can tell if they are open or shut. Or, if you're like me, just leave them dirty!

The other choice in tub enclosures is plastic. Too often we associate plastic with "cheap." In today's plastic world that is not true. Folding shower doors come in many beautiful colors—blue, green, pink, beige, gold, white, and white with a gold fleck. You can coordinate your existing color scheme with any of them or you can change the entire decor. I hope you'll choose to change the entire look of your bathroom.

I installed plastic doors in our first house. I almost wish I had them in this home. There is much to be said for them, but why not start with the negative things? They have a tendency to allow soap to stick to them, even more so than glass. You cannot use an abrasive cleaner on them or they will scratch, regardless of what you may be told.

But I have more to say in their favor than against them. First, they are easy to install due to their light weight. Glass panels are considerably heavier.

Second, the plastic shower doors fold back accordian style to allow total access to the tub area. When folded back they take up only about one foot, and they have a latch (much like a screen door hook and eye) that keeps them in position. This makes it easy to clean the tub or to bathe a child.

Third, the panels are crackproof and shatterproof. The plastic won't mold, mildew, or fade. (I have had trouble with mold forming at the bottom and top edges of glass panels, but maybe I don't clean them often enough.)

You should be able to find a good polyethylene (plastic) do-it-yourself tub enclosure for around $55.00. I recently saw a good tempered-glass enclosure at our local building discount store for $50.00, including all the slides and screws necessary for its installation. Compare those prices with the ones charged by a contractor who installs such enclosures. Then you will see how much your labor is worth. I picked two plumbing companies at random out of the phone book and asked for a quote. They wanted $85.00 and $90.00, respectively, to provide and install an enclosure, and that was using the cheapest materials. A good one can run well over $140.00 installed. See why we must do things ourselves?

To install a tub enclosure you will need a hacksaw, drill, level, and screwdriver. Be sure to measure the tub opening carefully before you purchase your enclosure. The average tub is five feet in length. If yours is longer or

shorter, mention this to the dealer. An odd-sized enclosure may cost you more money, but one that doesn't
fit at all is a total waste of money. So measure carefully,
right down to the last one-eighth of an inch.

To start, you will have to remove the existing shower
curtain rod. Very simple to do. Just take that trusty screwdriver, loosen the screws holding the rod and cover plate
in place, and remove it. If you have taken the screws out
of ceramic tile, you will have a few holes. Unfortunately,
I cannot tell you how to patch up a ceramic tile. Holes
made in one are there to stay. If you have a few extra
ceramic tiles, pry out the defective tiles and replace
them. Remember to grout them after setting them in the
mastic. If the holes are in plaster or plasterboard, they
are easily filled with spackle and painted to match your
color scheme.

There are different ways of installing the aluminum
frame that will hold the glass or plastic panels. I'll present two of them. Perhaps the directions that come with
your enclosure will be different. Follow the instructions
that come with it, because a manufacturer will not stand
behind his product unless you have installed it according to his specifications.

The only difference between the two types of
installation is in how you cut the bottom guide rail. One
way is to cut this piece, using a hacksaw, one inch shorter
than the tub opening. This is done on the assumption
that the side rails each measure one-half inch. If your
side rails are a different width, you will have to cut your
bottom rail accordingly. It is vitally necessary that the
bottom and sides fit as snugly together as possible. So
measure very carefully before you cut, as the slightest
gap will allow water to leak out when the shower is in use
(see Illustration 45).

The second way is to cut the bottom rail the exact length of the tub and insert it flush to both sides. Then in-

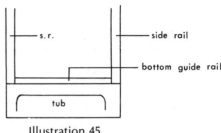

Illustration 45

stall the side rails on top of the bottom rail. This is the procedure I recommend for a beginner since it would be almost impossible to make a mistake in cutting. Only one measurement is necessary, and that is the length of the tub. You would not need to know the width of the side rails and then try to cut the bottom piece accordingly.

You will find drain holes in the bottom rail. When you install it be sure that the holes face into the tub. You certainly do not want the excess water to run out onto the floor. Usually you will find drain holes only in glass shower doors. The plastic units usually have a bottom track that is closed on top, so there's no trapped water, dirt, or soap residue to clean. I wish my glass shower doors had such a feature. Cleaning the track is enough to drive you insane.

It is not necessary to drill holes in the tub to hold the bottom rail. It is held in place by the two side pieces.

Mastic may be used to cement the bottom rail to the tub. I advise it, because no matter what some experts say, I think the bottom rail has a tendency to move slightly over the years. When purchasing mastic, be sure to buy one that is waterproof and made to adhere to porcelain (your tub) and metal (the guide strip). Ask your dealer to recommend the correct one for your particular installation.

Having installed the bottom rail, it is time to insert the side rails. The type of screws you use will depend on the surface of the walls in your bathroom. If you are going to install the side rails on ceramic tile, you will need a drill to make the screw holes. After marking with a pencil exactly where you want the holes, make a cross with Scotch tape on the marks. Drill through the tape and the tile should not split or crack. This trick also works on plaster walls any time you need to insert a nail (even for a picture). Plaster has a tendency to crack when a nail or screw is inserted into it.

Lay the side rail vertically on one wall. Fit it tightly to the bottom rail and line it up as straight as possible. Then, with that trusty level, make sure that the rail is vertical. Put the level up against the side rail and move the rail until the bubble is exactly centered. Mark the screw holes by putting a pencil tip through the three openings in the rail and making a dot directly on the wall. Remove the rail and start the holes, either with a drill, or, in the case of plasterboard, with an awl or a hammer and nail. After you have started the holes, replace the side rail and attach it firmly. Use the same procedure on the opposite side.

The only piece left to install is the top, or the header (as the pros call it). It, too, must be cut to fit snugly between both walls. Measure this cut at the height the piece will be installed in case the walls are not perfectly straight. Usually this piece is not bolted into the wall. The weight of the doors holds it in place. However, if the directions that come with your shower doors tell you to attach the header to the walls, do it!

Usually you cut the header to fit, and insert the

panels with the rollers on the top (if there is only one side that has rollers). Then you take this entire unit and set it in place on the bottom rail. This is a difficult procedure for a woman to handle alone. You are working with a great deal of bulk and, if you have chosen glass, a heavy weight. It's time to talk someone into helping you lift the unit into place so that it fits tightly on all four sides.

When placing the unit into the bottom rail, try not to slide it down the wall. You could scratch your wall. Instead, lean the unit slightly toward you and push it into place. Since it fits tightly, do not pull it away from the wall any more than is absolutely necessary—perhaps one-half inch or less.

Lay your level on top of the enclosure and make sure it is straight. Most door rollers may be adjusted to compensate for walls and tubs that are not perfectly level. However, if you followed the directions, there is no reason why the top piece should not be straight.

Now your new shower door is installed, and the bathroom has taken on an entirely new look. Right? So the rest of the room looks dowdy. Time for the next project to update the "throne room."

When I decided to redo the powder room, I couldn't pinpoint exactly what it was that annoyed me. I knew the room wasn't to my liking—the mirror was old, and the color of the sink and toilet was dated. I thought first about the walls. What kind of paper could I hang that would go with the existing tile? Had all the ceramic tile been beige (the predominant color), then a problem might not have existed. However, the previous owner had used a different color tile to "cap" the tiled area and again at the base. To make matters worse, he had inserted a patterned tile at random throughout the room. This made using a patterned wallpaper impossible.

I decided it was the ceramic tile that set me off. It ruined any decorating ideas I had. So I removed the tile—much to my husband's dismay. Any builder will tell you that adding ceramic tile to a bathroom or a powder room increases the value of a house by $300.00 or more. I couldn't agree more—but it's more important to like the tile.

Perhaps you are like me and do not like the existing tile in your bathroom. You can paint it, although most people would assume that this is an impossible task. It really isn't, but since I have never done it, I don't intend to go into great detail about it. All I'll say is that my local paint dealer sells an adhesive that will cover existing tile so that you can paint it; the adhesive builds up a bonding surface that the paint will adhere to. I cannot say whether or not the new paint will chip. I do know that the recommendation is to use enamel paint. But, again, check with the dealer. Only he "knows for sure."

Removing ceramic tile is no big deal. You will need a chisel and a hammer. Start from the top, put the chisel between the tile and the wall, and smack it with the hammer. If you don't like the tile, don't worry if it breaks. You're going to throw it away anyway. But if you want to save it, either to use elsewhere or to sell (which I did through our local swap-shop radio station), then you will have to take care in removing the tile. Try not to break or chip it. You'll probably break the first two or three tiles, but then you will get the hang of it. Insert the chisel behind the tile and pull it off gently.

Regardless of how carefully you remove the tile, you are going to make holes in the wall. If the walls are solid plaster, you will not have the same problem as you will have with plasterboard walls. I happen to have plasterboard walls and ended up with many holes and rips in them. Plaster does not fall out readily, although it will crack and chip.

Before I go into the repair of the walls, necessary before either tiling or papering, I wish to bring up one other point. That is what to do with the toilet paper holder. In many houses, it is positioned on the wall. Maybe you like yours there. If so, ignore this section. Ours was in the wall, and I was not happy with it. I found that the children would almost always touch the wall when removing the paper. There was always a dirty area surrounding the holder. Plus, it was in an inconvenient place. I have been in many homes where I had to search around to find the tissue holder (who wants to be an explorer when you're in need?). So, when I removed the tile, I also removed the chrome toilet paper frame. This left an immense hole in the wall that needed repairing.

Perhaps you might also want to remove the soap dish if it is recessed into the wall. It, too, may be set in an inconvenient place where people splash your walls when putting the bar of soap back. Soap dishes have a tendency to collect scum, and the chrome backing requires constant cleaning. I prefer a soap dish that sits directly on the counter top. It is easy to clean, and if there are small prongs on the bottom, the soap can dry out after being used. You can have an everyday one for the kids and a beautiful, ornate one for company.

If you have taken out either the tissue holder or the soap dish, you are going to be left with a large hole in the wall. Spackle won't fill the hole because there is no backing on which to apply it. So you will have to make your own backing—a simple procedure. There are two ways of doing this. Read them both and decide which sounds the easiest for you. Regardless of which you choose, the result will be the same.

Both methods require the same preparation. The hole left in the wall has jagged edges and is uneven in size. Take your keyhole saw and make the hole as even and as square (or rectangular, as the case may be) as possible.

For the first way, go to your local lumber dealer and purchase a small piece of plasterboard. Cut it to fit in the opening in the wall. Put a little glue around all four edges and set it into the hole. Place it in the opening about one-eighth of an inch *behind* the surface of the existing wall. Allow the glue to dry, and then cover the entire section with either spackle compound or a plaster mix. Smooth it out with your putty knife, let it dry, and sand it with medium-grade sandpaper. You will probably have to repeat the spackle coat two or more times to have a perfectly smooth patch. It is best to put on more spackle than necessary because it shrinks as it dries. Then the final sanding (with No. 0000 sandpaper) will make the patch "invisible."

The second way is to use a piece of wire screening. You prepare the wall in the same way as previously explained (cutting the jagged edges). Now, cut a piece of wire screening *larger* than the hole. Take a piece of string and tie it to the center of the screen. Put the screen into the hole but hold on to the string lest the wire disappear behind the wall. Now take a pencil (or any skinny piece of wood) and tie it to the string.

Pull the wire tightly against the back of the hole and tie the pencil in place to keep the wire screen flush against the back of the wall. The pencil must rest tightly against the front of the wall (see Illustration 46).

Then proceed to fill in the area exactly as you would have if you had used a piece of plasterboard. Naturally,

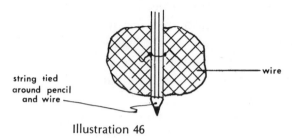

string tied
around pencil
and wire —

wire

Illustration 46

the area to be filled will be deeper, so it will require more filler. In this case I recommend using a plaster mix rather than the spackle compound. However, both will work equally well. Just the cost will differ. Due to the amount of spackle needed, using spackle will cost far more than using a plaster compound you mix yourself.

So whether the holes and cracks be large or small, they are repaired in somewhat the same way. And whether you intend to tile your bathroom or wallpaper it, all holes and cracks must first be repaired.

The walls are now smooth and ready for the ceramic tile. Before you purchase the tile, be sure you measure the area accurately. You can return any excess, but you may not be able to match the tile if you run out. I'll repeat the same thing I said in previous chapters—buy a little more than you need.

Tile comes in "runs" just as wallpaper does, and one run may differ from the next, even though the color and pattern are supposed to be the same. It is most annoying to me to be in the middle of a job and run out of materials. Don't let it happen to you. I learned this the hard way on my first attempt at home improvement.

First, a few facts about wall tile. The top piece of tile (assuming you are not going all the way up to the ceiling) is called the "cap." It can be the same color as the rest of the tile, or you may choose a contrasting color. The cap piece has a smooth rounded edge at the top. It is the finishing piece that fits snugly against the wall. No grouting is done above it (unless your wall is very uneven and a gap exists between the tile and the wall).

There also is a special piece of tile sold for the base (bottom piece). Again, it can either match or contrast with the rest of the tile. You will need base tiles because they curve outward from the wall and cover the line where the floor meets the wall. If you choose to contrast the cap and the base tiles to the rest of the ceramic, I would strongly suggest that these two types match. Or, the cap piece could be one color and the wall and base another, or vice-versa. (You, however, are decorating the room to *your* liking, so the color scheme is entirely up to you.)

If you intend to change the medicine cabinet, do so before tiling the walls. However, I will cover the laying of wall tile before I go into the replacement of a mirror or medicine cabinet. A little bit backwards, yes, but more of you are interested in tiling than in installing a new cabinet. If you do intend to install a new mirror or cabinet, then flip over a few pages to those instructions.

When purchasing tile for a bathroom, you will need to know the width of all the walls. Take your ruler and measure across the walls from one corner to the next. This figure will also give you the running feet of cap and base tile you'll need to buy. Write this figure down for future use.

Now decide how high up the wall you wish the tile to go. The usual height is approximately four and one-half feet from the floor. If you are going to have to cut around an existing medicine cabinet, you may wish to lower the height of the tile. Cutting ceramic tile is tricky, as I explained in the chapter on laying a ceramic floor, because it has a tendency to shatter. If you find that you will have a small gap between the mirror and where the tile would end, you could raise the height of the tile so that a full piece butts tightly to the cabinet or mirror.

When tiling a wall, try to plan ahead so that you do not have to cut tile needlessly. Measure one tile (usually four inches) and see if the height of the area you have decided to tile is divisible by the length of one tile. If not, and there is no medicine cabinet or mirror that you must conform to, raise or lower your top line so whole tiles are used.

If you must cut tiles, do not cut the cap or the base. All corrections should be made on the tiles that are next to the floor. The base tile covers the last tile laid and also hides any uneven cuts and gaps that may appear between the wall and the floor.

eye, to lay tile around a mirror cabinet. In such cases a cap tile is not used under the mirror but can be laid along the sides of the cabinet. The regular tiles are cut and put under the mirror so that the cut sides abut against the bottom of the mirror. Grout fills in any small gaps that may be visible. (See Illustration 47).

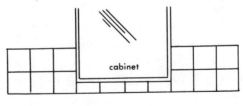

cabinet

Illustration 47

Now that you have decided how high you wish the tile to go, it is time to make your horizontal straight line. Place your level on the height mark you have decided upon and marked on the wall. Center the bubble and draw a line following the edge of the level. Continue around the room, using the level as your ruler (see Illustration 48).

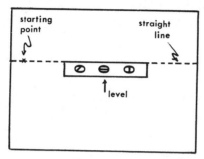

Illustration 48

Tile is laid from the top of the straight, horizontal line down to the floor. Don't worry, the tiles won't slip down the wall.

Once you have determined the horizontal line, you must mark the place where the first tile will be placed. The first tile is the most important one. You will be laying the cap pieces first. Measure the length of one wall, and divide it in half. Make a mark on the wall at the halfway point. Unless you are terribly lucky, the end pieces will have to be cut to fit the corners. You want the tiles on one corner to be the same width as the ones on the other corner of the same wall. This does not mean the end cuts should be the same all around the room—just that they should match on the same wall.

If you have chosen mosaic tile (one-inch square), the tiles are arranged on sheets and have spaces between them for the grout. However, if you have picked the larger tiles (four inches by four inches, which I recommend for a bathroom), the tiles are separate. Most tiles that are sold singly have small protrusions on each side that space the tile automatically. These protrusions are called lugs. Even if you have to pay a little bit more for a tile with lugs, it is worth it in the long run. It is very hard to space tile by eye.

Some bathroom tile is even pregrouted. Grouting is necessary only around the fixtures and where the floor and wall meet.

Spread the mastic on the wall about one-fourth of an inch below the top line. Keep your center starting point mark visible. Take one piece of the cap tile and place it over the center mark so half the tile is on one side and half on the other (see Illustration 49). Continue along the horizontal line and set the rest of the cap pieces. The end pieces will probably have to be cut to fit the corners.

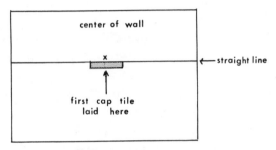

Illustration 49

Spread the mastic and set the tile across the wall one row at a time. Continue laying tile all the way to the floor. After you finish a row, check to make sure that the seams are perfectly vertical and horizontal (again, use the level). The base pieces are laid on top of the bottom row of tile. The base piece must lie flat on the floor; it is the finishing piece.

When cutting the pieces that will fit into the corners of the room (vertically), follow the instructions for tile cutting given in the chapter on laying ceramic floor tile.

After you have laid the base pieces, there is only one more step—grouting between the tiles. This, too, has been covered in the chapter on ceramic tile floors. The procedure is exactly the same.

Now that the walls are tiled, you have increased the value of your home by $300.00, more or less, depending on the size of the room.

If you have a tub or shower area, you will want to tile that also. Tile in this area is installed in the same way. You will have to loosen the shower head and the faucet to fit the tile behind them. Using your tile snippers, cut the tile that will fit around the pipe. Be careful not to snip off too much because the cover plate must fit on top of the tile. Otherwise, you will have a leak behind the wall.

Do not use grout along the edge where the tile meets the tub, and around the shower and faucet heads and recessed soap holder. Use waterproof caulking made for tubs and showers. It comes in a squeeze tube. Caulking prevents water leakage behind these units. One company manufactures sheets of tile that are two feet by two feet and are designed to fit perfectly above most standard-size tubs. They also make shower surrounds that fit the four most popular sizes. These units can be installed directly over properly sealed drywall. They extend up the wall seventy-two inches, but there are extension packages for tiling all the wall to the ceiling. I strongly recommend the latter for either a tub area or a shower stall. In fact, it really looks nice (and makes for easy cleaning) if you tile the ceiling too. Tile the ceiling exactly as you would a floor.

There is one other product you might wish to look into when tiling a shower enclosure or a tub area—sheets of either Formica or MarLite that are sized to fit the space. One company also puts out five-foot by six-foot murals suitable for tub or shower stalls. Some of these panels may be applied directly over ceramic tile walls. In fact, this is going to be my next project. I have looked over these products carefully and checked their directions. They are not complicated to install and have the added benefit of not requiring grout.

With new shower doors installed and new walls contemplated, you may wish to change that outdated medicine cabinet. As I stated before, replace the cabinet or mirror before tiling the walls. If there is only a mirror on your bathroom wall, you are missing some valuable storage area. Even in a powder room a cabinet is a handy place to store extra soap, a comb, lipstick, and other bathroom necessities. In a master bathroom there is nothing nicer than a medicine cabinet that has a solid mirror in the center and two side doors that are also mirrored. By arranging the doors at an angle, you can see your hair and face from all sides.

Replacing an old medicine cabinet is not complicated. There are two types of medicine cabinets. One is recessed, meaning that it is sunk into the wall. The other type is flush mounted. It is hung directly on the wall and does not require any cutting into the wall. Naturally it is easier to hang a flush-mounted cabinet on the wall if you have only removed a mirror or a smaller-size recessed cabinet. However, a flush-mounted cabinet stands out from the wall quite a bit more than does the recessed type. In a small powder room, this could be undesirable.

It certainly would be easier, if you have decided to remove a recessed cabinet, to replace it with one of equal size. Medicine cabinets are held in place with screws on the sides. Take the old cabinet out and insert the new one, making sure it is level both on the top and the sides. Always be sure to follow the manufacturer's instructions when installing a cabinet.

You may wish to install a larger cabinet than the existing one. This entails a little more work since you will have to enlarge the opening. Measure the back of the cabinet and, using your keyhole saw, cut a hole in the wall as close as possible to the measurements of the cabinet back. It is better to have the hole slightly larger (but only by about one-fourth of an inch) than to make it too small. The cabinet must be centered between the wood studs behind the wall because you will have to screw the cabinet into them.

There are many different ways of determining the placement of studs in the wall. Some people will suggest knocking on the wall until you hear a "solid" sound, meaning you have hit the stud, while a "hollow" sound indicates empty space behind the wall. Others suggest drilling holes in the wall, starting sixteen and three-quarters inches from one end of the wall. They assume that the studs are spaced sixteen inches apart, on center. Of course, you will have to repair the holes you have made in the wall while making your search. The best, and easiest method of locating studs is with a stud-finder, which you can purchase from your hardware dealer. A stud-finder works like a compass. Hold the stud-finder along the base of the wall about one-half inch above the floor. The needle will move when it passes over the large nails in the base of the stud. The stud runs vertically up the wall from this point.

Again, I quote Douglas Tuomey of the *Chicago Tribune:* "If you're not fortunate enough to have the studs so situated, you'll have to improvise. After the hole is made, you may have to cut out a section of one stud and install a false stud a few inches to one side.

"This may be accomplished by nailing two short horizontal two-by-fours [pieces of wood] approximately sixteen inches long into both sides of the top and bottom exposed ends of the middle stud just cut out. The other ends should be toenailed [putting a nail in on an angle through one piece of wood into the adjoining piece] into the next closest stud on each side.

"Now a vertical piece of two-by-four should be toenailed into the two horizontal members, spaced to allow just enough room to insert the rear of the cabinet." (The explanations in brackets are mine, not Mr. Tuomey's.)

Perhaps you've removed a large recessed cabinet and have chosen one that is smaller. Regardless of whether you have chosen a flush or a recessed model, all or some of the space must be filled in. Nail two-by-fours onto the existing vertical studs on either side of the cavity. Nail one next to another until you have built in the opening to conform to the size of the cabinet. Then you will have to build up the wall with plasterboard and spackle so it is even with the existing wall. I explained previously how to fix a hole in plaster or plasterboard (as when removing a toilet paper holder).

If the cabinet you removed was flush mounted, you will have no trouble hanging another flush-mounted cabinet. With this type of cabinet, it is not necessary to cut the wall. Just unscrew the old cabinet and replace it with the new. It may be necessary to remove some tiles (if they are already present) if the new cabinet is larger than the old. Cut the edge tiles so they fit snugly against the cabinet and grout around the edges.

Last of the major projects is replacing that ugly sink that stands on legs. It is technically called a wall-hung lavatory. Don't let the plumber's language scare you. It sounds more impressive and, therefore, more expensive to work with. A sink is a sink, whether it's called a lavatory or an ugly sink on legs.

Wouldn't it be nice to have a cabinet sink? This type

of sink is among the easiest of all bathroom fixtures to install, although a plumber may tell you differently (that's how they make their money). I really don't mean to knock plumbers. They are vitally necessary when a major disaster hits your plumbing. But you don't need to support them when you can "do it yourself."

Even the use of the common plunger when the toilet is stopped up may save you a service call. At least try it before you make that call. By the same token, some commercial drain cleaner may unclog a drain if the problem is a hair ball. Use the drain cleaner before you call for help. Money saved is money earned!

Back to the installation of a cabinet sink. By purchasing one at a building supplies discount center, you can save quite a bit of money, but a sink still is not cheap. If you are going to install one, buy a good unit that will last. However, you will find that the quoted price for a cabinet sink usually does not include the fixture (the faucet for water). In some "come-on" ads the price may not even include the sink! So, when comparing prices be sure you are comparing the same offering.

You can use your old faucet, but it is probably corroded from years of use. A new faucet can be single levered (one control that you move from right to left to get the temperature desired) or double levered (one handle for cold and another for hot). Today, most people prefer the single handle. Be sure that you purchase a faucet that will fit the hole or holes in the cabinet top. It is advisable to buy both at the same place so you are assured of a perfect fit.

The first and most important step is to turn off the water on the existing sink. Most homes built within the last ten years have a shut-off valve below the sink. It is simply a handle that turns off the water. If there isn't one in your bathroom, you will have to turn off the water at the main valve. Locate your water meter and you will see a round handle next to it. Turn this off by tightening it. Then turn on the faucet. Let it run for a few minutes to empty the pipes.

Should the hot water keep running, it is necessary to turn off the valve on the hot water heater. In a basement, this valve is located overhead and is attached to the heater. Usually this step is not necessary. Turning off the water at the main switch should cut off all water throughout the house. Cutting it off at the local valve will turn off the water only in that particular room. No matter where your valve is located, find it and turn the water off. Otherwise you will have a major flood and clean-up job.

A wall-hung sink (lavatory) is easy to remove. Once you have turned off the water supply, you must remove the faucets. Start with your head (and hands) under the sink. You will see a flat piece of metal that is connected to the stopper in the drain hole in the center of the sink. It is attached to a vertical piece of notched metal. Disconnect this piece and save it. In fact, save all pieces you take off—you may need them later.

Using your pliers (or socket wrenches, if you have them), loosen the screws that connect the pipes to the hot and cold water faucets and also the one hooked on to the drain. Remove them so that the sink is no longer connected to any pipes.

A wall-hung sink is usually set on the wall by means of a metal plate that is attached to the wall. To remove the sink, all you need to do is lift it up and then out. You can remove the legs first for ease in handling, but it is not necessary. Actually, leaving the legs on makes it easier to sell the unit. By selling it you have reduced the cost of your new cabinet. I speak from experience. I sold a powder room sink through the local swap-shop radio program and will soon have another for sale.

The metal plate is attached to the wall with either bolts or screws. Remove them and the plate will fall off. Now you are ready to install the new cabinet.

Set the cabinet against the wall, centering it beneath the medicine cabinet or mirror. Should there be a backing piece on the cabinet (most do not have one), it may have holes in it for the pipes to come through. Make sure that the holes and pipes are lined up. If there is a backing with no holes in it, you will have to cut holes, using the keyhole saw. Save time, labor, and money by purchasing a cabinet sink that has no back. Who but a nosey person would ever look anyway? Paint the wall behind the cabinet, or wallpaper it.

Should you have to add piping (if the new fixtures are spaced differently from the existing ones), buy the flexible kind. A plumber uses what is called "rigid pipe," which must be cut to exact measurements and is difficult for an amateur to install. Flexible piping can be cut to within an inch or two of the necessary length and then bent to fit. Connect it with the same nuts and bolts you removed from the original sink.

Having put your cabinet exactly where you want it, you should fasten it to the wall. I say "should" because it entails finding a stud in the wall and nailing the back of the cabinet to it. I did not nail the cabinet I installed to the wall, and it has stayed put for many years. After all, how many people are going to pull or push it?

Reconnect the water faucets (or faucet, as the case may be) in exactly the same way that you disconnected them, except in reverse. Attach the drain stopper to the metal piece that you removed, and make sure that it is affixed to the "U" tube under the sink. Connect the hot water pipe to the correct (left) valve and the cold water pipe to its valve. Tighten the bolts and turn on the water. If you had to turn off the valve at the hot water heater, don't forget to turn it back on.

What an addition a cabinet sink has made to your bathroom!

There is one other major fixture in the bathroom that I didn't cover—and it surely is the most important. That is the toilet. Please don't try the installation of a new toilet yourself. This is one time that a plumber is absolutely necessary. Unless the unit is properly installed on the stack (that big hole in the floor), you run a great risk of sewer gas seeping out. Not only does sewer gas have a terrible odor, but it is combustible. This installation should be done only by a licensed plumber, since he knows how to properly seal the opening.

You can change the toilet seat, however, with no trouble at all. Even if the bowl is white, you can change its looks by installing a new seat and cover. Usually an old toilet seat is the worse for wear. All you do is remove the two screws that hold the existing seat and replace the old seat with a new one.

Just a few more ideas for the bathroom—decorating, not remodeling. In place of a curtain or window shade in my powder room, I opted for chenille balls strung on a thread. The room is done in red, white, and black, so I purchased strands of the chenille in these colors. I alternated the colors and cut the strands different lengths. Not only is the effect different, but it ties the room together. You could try the same idea with beads. Or, if you have wallpaper in the bathroom, cover the window shade in the same pattern. Then hang a valance of material (contrasting or the same print) across the top of the window, and drape it slightly down the sides. There are so many different ideas for sprucing up a bathroom other than the old "change the towels" routine.

You might want to try wall-to-wall carpeting (washable, of course) rather than tile to cover an unsightly floor. Buy it in a length and width slightly larger than your room and cut it to fit. It is not expensive. Directions for cutting are included with the carpeting and are not at all difficult. Mail-order houses often carry a completely color-coordinated line of carpeting, towels, seat covers, soap dishes, and even soap. You can mix or match, according to your preference.

Now that you have completed one bathroom, I'll bet you can't wait to get started on another!

Basement Remodeling

What is an unfinished basement but a catchall for everything that you don't wish to put into the attic or crawlspace? I'll bet that you could give away or sell almost everything in your basement. An unfinished cement basement floor constantly sheds cement dust. You carry it up the stairs on your shoes and deposit it throughout the house. Unfinished wooden stairs have a tendency to splinter and crack, making them dangerous to walk on. If these aren't enough reasons for finishing a basement, let me present a few more. If you have young children or teen-agers, what better place could you have for them to entertain their friends? If you have young children a basement is a natural playroom; you can put up a train set, lay out a play kitchen for your daughter, or let the kids ride their tricycles without fear of damage to your house.

Anyone who has teen-agers (and I have four) knows

how loudly they play radios and record players and then try to talk over the deafening noise—not to mention the wild dancing. Who needs this in the living room, or even in the family room, for that matter? Teen-agers also enjoy a pool table or a ping-pong table. Best of all, you will find teen-agers behave better in a finished basement than in a bare one.

The use of a basement is not limited to the children of the family. My husband and I use the basement any time we entertain more than ten people. Our bar is there and an old rinky-dink piano. We find we have a much better time entertaining a group (frequently thirty or more people) downstairs than upstairs. Our friends are much less inhibited there than they are in the living room with the white carpeting, where they do not feel they have the freedom to move about.

Last but not least, I use the basement for family dinners on special occasions—birthdays, Thanksgiving, and graduation. Would you believe even baptism? Where else can we seat twenty-four people around one table except in the basement?

Having presented some reasons why I think you would be happier with a finished basement, I will give you some of the options available for finishing it. Again, remember that the ideas are as unlimited as your imagination. You can create anything from an old-time barroom to an ultramodern twenty-first century room. The ideas are yours. I'll try to provide the technical information.

The first basement my husband and I had was done in "Matt Dillon style." We used tongue-and-groove, one-inch thick, solid walnut boards. We also had a solid butternut ceiling (too expensive today). By cutting out sections of the paneling, inserting Old West pictures with cactus plants below them, and adding swinging café doors, we recreated yesteryear. Our current basement is done in blond wood paneling and white ceiling tile that looks like wood.

I have seen basements finished to resemble a fisherman's cove, a travel bureau (by covering the walls with the posters supplied by the airlines), and a rustic barn, and some that have no theme whatsoever. You can panel halfway up the wall and use stucco, wallpaper, or burlap above the paneling. It all depends on what you want.

This chapter will deal with erecting studs for walls, the different types of wall coverings available, plus purchasing and installing wood paneling. I'll also include instructions on how to build a simple bar. Laying a floor has already been covered in a previous chapter. These instructions also apply if you wish to make a den or office out of an unused bedroom or to update an older family room. In fact, paneling is frequently used today in the living room. The installation is the same, with minor adjustments according to the room.

Paneling can turn a so-so master bedroom into a truly magnificent room and transform a dining room or a kitchen into a totally new room. It can even be used in a bathroom (except in the tub or shower area).

So, as you can see, even though this chapter is on creating a finished basement, the ways you can use wood paneling are almost limitless and care and upkeep are almost nonexistent. A wipe-down with a wood-care product once or twice a year is all that is necessary to keep it looking new for years. It doesn't fingerprint easily and can be touched-up with a matching paint should it chip or crack.

Before you look for paneling, go down to your basement and look it over carefully. Make up your mind about the theme you wish to follow, or if you don't want a theme, what improvements, such as paneled walls and a tile floor, you want to make. If you want a bar, decide where you are going to place it. Study your laundry and furnace area and see how you are going to close it off, for you surely don't want it visible when entertaining (you have to have a place to throw all the junk). If you have a bilevel home, you may want to install louvered doors (for air circulation) in front of the appliances and panel the entire room. Bilevels usually have a partial basement and every little bit of space counts.

Ranch houses and two-story homes normally have a full basement. Using the "I" beam (the steel or heavy wood piece that runs overhead the full length of the room and supports the first floor) as a center guide, you may wish to make three rooms out of one basement. You can have a laundry-furnace-water heater-tool room occupying one part of the basement. Another part could be utilized as a poolroom, office, or child's playroom, complete with train set up. Use the remaining part as the finished entertaining area (see Illustration 50).

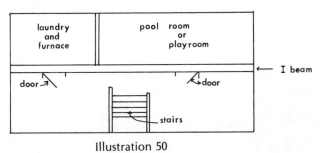

Illustration 50

Lay out the design of the room on paper, then measure the walls you intend to panel. On your drawing, mark where doors are to be hung and the width that you want them. When measuring for doors, keep one thing in mind. A prehung standard-size door is much cheaper than one that has to be made to order. You will need paneling to go above the doors, although if you have chosen panels that come in sheets, you can cut one sheet to go above two or three doors, thereby saving money.

There is one last very important thing to check. Do you have enough electrical outlets along the wall? You will want to plug in lamps, a record player, and maybe a television. If you intend to serve food downstairs, you will need outlets to plug in warming trays. Look up at the ceiling. One overhead light is not going to be enough to light an entire basement. Don't forget that you are going to need extra outlets behind a bar (if you intend to have one) for a blender, ice crusher, clock (you do want everyone to leave on time!), and maybe a novelty lamp.

Do not try to do the electrical work yourself. The danger of electrocution is immense. Improper wiring has caused numerous fires in homes. Plan where you want your outlets and overhead fixtures and hire a reputable electrician to install them.

Electricians are not cheap, but they are worth every cent they charge. You can figure on spending roughly $20.00 for each double outlet needed, $40.00 for a double switch plate (the on-off unit on the wall), $20.00 for a single switch, and $10.00 to hang an overhead fixture. These are only estimates, since prices differ in different communities, but they give you an idea of the expense involved. The electrician does his work after you have installed the studs and furring strips but before you put up the paneling.

Now, with layout in hand, visit your building supplies dealers. Notice, I say "dealers." Go to three or four, from the local lumberyard to the large home improvement discount center. Compare products and prices.

Check the newspapers for sales, but be sure that if the price is less at one place than another, the quality is the same.

Lumber, plywood, and paneling are priced according to grade, quality, thickness, and type of wood. Lumber comes in many forms. The first is called solid stock, framing lumber. This includes two-inch by four-inch boards you will use as studs for the basement wall frame. Buy only perfectly straight lengths of lumber as paneling will not lie flush on a warped piece (one that is bent or curved). Do not purchase green lumber (fresh lumber) because it has a tendency to shrink as it dries, and any nails driven into it will push out through the drywall or paneling. This is a common cause for nail popping in your home. Ask to see only kiln-dried lumber (and closely inspect each piece). It costs a bit more but, believe me, it is worth it. Usually each piece is stamped "Kiln-Dried."

Green lumber is not sold in most places today. The government stepped in and set up standards for the industry to follow. Therefore, a two-by-four does not measure exactly two inches by four inches. As it dried, it shrank. Also, to provide a smooth finish and to get more footage from each board, two-by-fours are further reduced in size. So the actual measurements of a "two-by-four" are one and one-half by three and one-half inches. You must keep this in mind when ordering studs and also when placing them on the wall. In other words, what you buy ain't what you get.

Lumber is also classified as hardwood and softwood. Some hardwoods are maple, walnut, birch, and cherry. Softwoods include fir, pine, and cedar.

An easy way to differentiate between these two types is: hardwoods come from trees that have leaves and softwoods come from trees with needles. But don't be misled by the names; redwood and mahogany are classified as hardwoods but are extremely "soft" woods to work with (meaning the nails go in easily).

Plywood is another form of lumber. In essence, all plywood consists of is thin sheets of wood that are laminated (glued) together, one on top of another. By reversing the grain (pattern) on each sheet as it is glued to the next, the manufacturer ends up with a very strong piece of wood. Plywood, like prefinished panels, comes in four-by-eight-foot sheets. An added plus: a sheet four feet by eight feet is nearly always that size. A one-half-inch thickness of plywood has the approximate strength of a one-inch thick piece of solid lumber.

Plywood comes in both interior and exterior finishes. Naturally the exterior finish is more expensive since it is laminated with waterproof coating to resist moisture. If you intend to panel a bathroom, you will need exterior-finish plywood and a water-resistant adhesive. For any other job inside the house, the interior kind is fine.

Plywood is graded according to appearance and use. The three most common grades are: 1.   A-C grade; this means the panel has a good face (front) and an unfinished back. It is laminated with exterior glue for outside use. 2.   A-D grade; this grade is for interior use only. It has a good face but will have knots (holes) in the back. 3.   C-D grade; this is plywood that is generally unfinished on both sides. It may be sold under the name of plyscore. You would not use it on walls or floors where appearance counts. An example of its use would be as a subfloor in an attic.

The grade is plainly printed on the back of each sheet of plywood. When choosing plywood be sure to look at the back and check the grade so you know where you can use it. Knowing the grade will also help you when comparing prices for seemingly identical products at different stores.

Next we come to paneling. This is probably what you will choose when redoing a room. There are two basic types of paneling that you should be familiar with. The first is called hardboard. You are probably more familiar with its other names, Masonite and pegboard. It has many uses that will be covered in the last chapter of this book. Pegboard comes in different colors; it can lend itself to any decor. Naturally, the plain, tan finish is the least expensive and is probably what you would choose for a garage or other unimportant area. But pegboard also comes in colors to harmonize with any scheme. One manufacturer has panels with holes in the top half only (for hooks). This type could be used in a child's bedroom. Then he or she could easily hang posters, prom bids, and so on. Pegboard comes with one-eighth-inch and one-fourth-inch holes. Use the board with larger holes for a work area (for heavy tools) or in a garage.

Technically, hardboard paneling is nothing more than wood chips and fibers that have been glued together to form a sheet and then made to resemble real boards by printing a design on the sheet. Hardboard also can be imprinted to resemble leather, marble, stone, and cork. But there is one very important thing to remember about hardboard: do not use it below grade (beneath the outside grass level). One sheet, yes, above a work bench or a sewing table. But never panel a basement with it. Due to its composition, it will expand and contract with changes in humidity. If it expands, it may buckle. If it contracts (shrinks), it may pull away from the adjoining sheet or the wall. Hardboard does not lend itself to being covered with wallpaper, grass cloth, canvas, burlap, or other covering. Its dimension variation makes permanent seaming impossible. This is true also of the hardboard that is imprinted to resemble wood or any other finish.

Hardboard has another use that is well worth mentioning. It can be used for underlayment on an uneven floor that you wish to tile. Underlayment is simply the term for a four-by-four-foot sheet of hardboard, one-fourth of an inch thick, that is nailed or stapled onto an existing, but rotted or uneven, floor before tile is put down. As long as you are working above grade level, you will have no problem with dimensional changes due to moisture absorption.

Hardboard comes in two grades. I hope I'm not confusing you with too much technical information, but it is vital that you know the difference before making any purchase. To "act" dumb in order to get help from the dealer is one thing, but to actually be dumb is another. Unless you know all the different types of wood and wood imitations, it is all too easy to be taken in when comparing prices and materials.

The first grade of hardboard is called *standard*. Standard hardboard is strictly for interior use. It cannot be used below grade level.

The second grade of hardboard is called *tempered*. This means it has been treated for exterior use and can withstand the elements. This is the type that would be used in a bathroom. Even though the bathroom is inside the home, paneling should be waterproof because of the moisture from the shower and tub. However, don't be confused by the word "tempered." This hardboard still cannot be used below grade level.

Back to the prefinished paneling. Hardboard was the first. The second type is made up of plywood veneers. The word "veneer" simply means that an expensive piece of wood has been glued onto a less expensive piece of wood backing. The face of the paneling may come from one of a variety of trees: mahogany, walnut, cherry, cedar, and so on. The backing is an inexpensive wood. An example would be a panel with a walnut face and a fir backing.

You will find that panels that have a hardwood veneer will differ in color, grain, and intensity. To me, that is what makes them so beautiful. One is not just like another, unless you special order them "in sequence"—and will that cost a fortune!

Plywood veneer has one thing in common with hardboard. It also can have an expensive wood-grain finish imprinted on a cheaper piece of wood veneer. This is called a "photo finish." If you purchase a plywood veneer (sometimes called hardwood), be sure you ask if the veneer is a photograph finish or the real wood. Naturally, the simulated wood will cost less than the real thing, but each will wear the same, so let your taste be your guide.

Most prefinished panels come in sheets four feet wide by eight feet long (called four-by-eight sheets). They are available in several thicknesses. The thinnest sold is one-eighth of an inch thick. This thin sheet is the cheapest, but it also is the easiest to buckle or fold. Unless you are installing panels against an existing plaster or plasterboard wall, steer clear of these thin panels. They are great on an upstairs wall, but when used against a stud wall in a basement, they should be backed up with plasterboard, and this is double work and more expense. Although the cost is more per panel, you would be wise to keep to the one-fourth-inch thickness, which will not dent, buckle, or crack under normal usage.

Paneling does come in sizes other than four-by-eight feet, but the larger panels are much more expensive. Besides, large panels are unwieldy to work with. Some panels come in a sixteen-inch width. They require more labor to install, but are easy for a woman to handle. You may also find panels sold in four-foot by seven-foot sheets because of the popularity of the seven-foot basement ceiling.

I have tried to present the different types of hardboard, hardwood, and paneling so that you will understand the pros and cons of each. The final choice rests solely with you. Check more than one store before you buy, for you are going to live with the paneling for a long, long time.

If you are going to panel an existing plaster or plasterboard wall, you will not need to put up studs, assuming the wall is straight and even. The panels can be installed directly over the existing surface. Although most people think they have to nail the panels up, this is not necessarily true. Today there are a variety of adhesives available, so you may be able to glue the panels directly to the wall. Ask your dealer for the correct adhesive for your particular paneling and walls.

Your dealer will also sell you a caulking gun (see Illustration 51). A tube of mastic is inserted into it, and as you squeeze the trigger, the mastic comes out in a thin strip. You spread it on the wall in a zig-zag pattern. (I would advise you to nail the four corners of the panel to the wall about three inches in from each side, so as not to crack or splinter the panel.) The nails are added insurance that the paneling will adhere. The nail holes will be covered on the top by the molding and on the bottom by the baseboard.

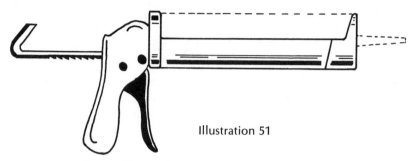

Illustration 51

You will need enough baseboard and base shoe or quarter round to go around the entire room. Also, you will want a piece of molding, called "cove," to cover the joint where the paneling meets the ceiling. The amount needed is determined by the lengths of the walls. For example, if the room is fifteen feet by twenty feet, you will need seventy running feet each of baseboard, base shoe, and cove (thirty feet for the two fifteen-foot walls and forty feet for the two twenty-foot ones). Ordering these items to match the paneling is expensive; it is much cheaper to purchase pine moldings and stain them yourself. I also recommend using cove in each corner of the room, running it vertically from ceiling to floor where the panels meet to form a right angle.

This is primarily a chapter on finishing a basement, so I will now cover the purchase and use of studs. Studs are pieces of lumber that measure one-by-two inches, one-by-three inches, or two-by-four inches in width and thickness. Thus their common names: one-by-twos, one-by-threes, and two-by-fours. You can have them cut to whatever length you need. The thin studs (called furring strips) are used on the ceiling. From my experience, you can forget the one-by-twos altogether. They split easily and are very difficult for an amateur to correctly install. Use one-by-threes on the ceiling and two-by-fours for the wall.

Basement walls are made of concrete. They are rough and uneven, and you cannot put paneling directly on top of them. So you must stud out the wall before paneling. Be sure that you purchase perfectly straight boards. Warped, or bent, ones will cause your wall to be uneven. Check them carefully and return any that are not perfect. A studded wall will look like Illustration 52.

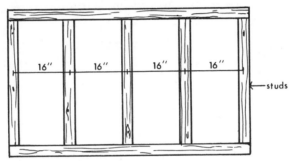

Illustration 52

Some do-it-yourself books recommend nailing the studs directly to the concrete. I don't recommend this at all, for two reasons. First, a basement wall is rarely even. If the studs are not in a perfect line, your panels will not fit together neatly, and this would necessitate "shimming out" behind your studs. To shim out means to insert small pieces of wood between the wall and the stud until the stud is straight. I think this takes too much time and effort.

Second, and most important for a woman, it is dangerous and difficult to nail studs directly into a concrete wall, even using the most popular method, the power nail (Ram set) gun. It is all too easy for a nail to ricochet off the wall and go haywire. Many years ago one of my neighbors was using one which misfired. The nail flew out and struck him in the heart, and he died before he even knew what hit him.

If you use the power nail gun to nail the base stud to the floor, take these precautions. Be sure when renting such a gun that it has a safety plate that extends all around the unit. Never remove the safety plate from the gun. Wear safety glasses. Lay the safety plate perfectly flat against the two-by-four. Never shoot the nail in at an angle. It must go straight in; otherwise you are inviting disaster. The trigger is difficult to operate, and the entire unit is unwieldy and difficult to control.

When it is necessary to nail directly into concrete, as in the stud base and when erecting a bar, I use a tool called a Fas-N-It (see Illustration 53). There is no chance of an accident when you use this tool, but it does take a lot of muscle. Using it is very simple. A nail (long and hard enough to penetrate a two-by-four and still go into the concrete) is inserted into the bottom opening. This will automatically push the plunger up a few inches from the top of the unit. With the nail in the unit, lay the Fas-N-It on top of the stud you wish to secure. Hold it with one hand and use your other hand to wield a hammer. You'll need a heavy duty hammer and a lot of sweat. Pound that nail in until it is flush (even) with the board.

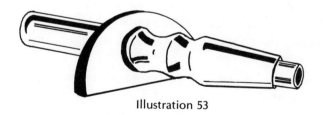

Illustration 53

The first step in studding out a wall is to make an accurate line on the floor with a chalk line. I advise keeping the stud base away from the wall about one inch. This way you will have no problem with an uneven wall, and the air space creates a natural barrier against damp or leaking walls. You could insert insulation batting between the wall and the paneling, but this is not necessary.

Measure out from the wall one inch at both ends. Make a mark on the floor. Fasten down the chalk line (with Scotch or masking tape) directly on the mark. Pull your chalk line out as you walk to the opposite end of the room. Set it down on that mark, pull it tight, and snap it in place. You will now have a straight line, even though the wall itself may be uneven. Repeat this procedure for the other walls in the room (see Illustration 54).

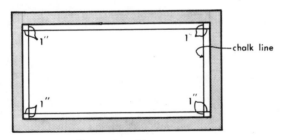

Illustration 54

Set the two-by-fours along (and inside of) this line. The four-inch side rests on the floor. Regardless of whether you have chosen to use the power nail gun or the Fas-N-It tool, you will nail these pieces to the floor the same way. The nails (cut nails used especially for concrete installation) are installed every four inches along the length of the two-by-fours. Continue around the room, except where there are door openings and underneath stairs.

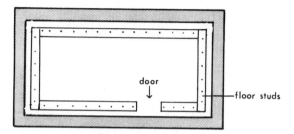

Illustration 55

As you will notice from the illustration, it is not necessary to miter the corners (cut the boards on an angle). The base studs can be put down at right angles to each other.

The next step is to install the two-by-fours that go along the ceiling, thus completing the framework for the vertical studs. The procedure is exactly the same as for the floor. Measure out one inch from the walls at the ceiling level, make a mark at either end of the wall on the ceiling or the joists (the beams that support the first floor) and snap the chalk line. On the walls that are at a right angle to the joists you will have no problem. However, you may have a problem on the walls that run parallel with the joists. The last joist may not be close enough to the wall. In that case you would have to nail additional two-by-fours to the end joist(s) so that they rest on the concrete wall or are nailed to the piece of wood (sill plate) that lies against the concrete. These would be nailed all around the room. Otherwise you will not have a nailing base for the top framing piece.

Nail the top framing pieces onto the ceiling joists, following the straight chalk line. You will need to continue above doors or window openings.

Now for the actual studding. Measure accurately the distance between the overhead stud, sometimes called the top plate, and the base. This is the measurement of the vertical studs you will install. Cut your two-by-fours this length. Buy or rent a power saw for this job, and be sure to use safety glasses. The (wo)man hours saved, plus the wear and tear on your body, are worth the cost.

The studs are placed along the wall every sixteen inches on center, and you will need one at the end of each wall. Therefore, in the corners you will have two together. Corner studs are necessary even though the space between the corner stud and the next stud is only a few inches.

When the vertical studs are cut, start at one corner of the room to install them. This is done by a process known as toenailing. Place the stud on the base so that the thin two-inch side faces you and the four-inch side is at a right angle to the wall. Toenailing means taking a nail, inserting it into the vertical stud on an angle, and pounding it into the base. Put another nail into the stud on the opposite side (see Illustration 56).

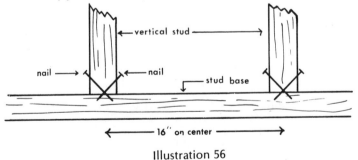

Illustration 56

Since you want the studding perfectly straight, it is time to use the level. With the bottom of the stud firmly attached to the base, run your level up the stud. When the bubbles show that the piece is perfectly straight, repeat the toenailing process to fasten the vertical stud to the top framing piece. Continue around the room, placing a stud every sixteen inches on center (that is, sixteen inches from the center of one stud to the center of the next stud). Yes, it does take time, but the final result is worth it.

You must frame door jambs (openings) and windows entirely, whether or not they are sixteen inches from the last stud (see Illustration 57).

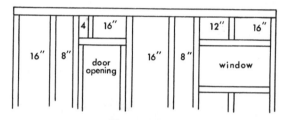

Illustration 57

When framing a door opening you must know the type of door (swinging, bifold, bi-pass, and so on) you are going to use and get the rough opening measurement from your materials dealer. A door two feet, six inches wide by six feet, eight inches high requires a rough opening of two feet, eight inches wide by six feet, nine inches high.

Now to prepare the paneling. Since sheets of paneling usually measure four feet by eight feet, and most basement ceilings are only seven feet high, it is necessary to cut the paneling to size. I prefer to use a power saw. However, whether you choose a power saw or a hand saw, use a fine-toothed blade when cutting paneling. This prevents chipping.

Measure the distance from the outside of the top framing piece to the outside of the bottom one (in other words, from the ceiling level to the floor). This will be the length of your first piece of paneling and all those to follow.

Lay the panel on the floor and mark the correct length on the back of it. Draw a straight line across the panel. Lay the panel across two very sturdy supports in order to cut it. The best supports are "horses." You have probably seen horses guarding a road under repair or closing off a street in a school zone. However, you can use two stepladders or even two very steady chairs. The main consideration is to have the panel supported on both ends and at a height that is convenient for you.

Paneling should be cut with the face (finished) side down when using a power saw. This prevents any chance of scratching the face and will also give a smoother edge. If you use a hand saw, the face of the panel should be up. Take your time when cutting. Do not force the saw. Forcing the saw may either tear the sheet or pull the saw away from the cutting line, thereby marring the surface.

Start paneling at the left end of a wall at the corner. Fit the panel into the corner as best you can. Using one nail, attach it to the first stud at the top lefthand side. Drive this nail in securely, but not tightly. In other words, do not put it all the way in—just far enough to hold the panel in place. Now use the level. Place it against the edge of the right side of the panel. Move the panel until the bubbles in the level are dead center all the way down the sheet. This assures that the first panel is perfectly straight. After ascertaining the straightness of the panel, insert another nail at the top righthand side. Make one more check with the level to be sure that the panel is straight vertically. Then pound in the two nails flush with the wood, being careful not to mar the finish of the panel. This is where the nail set comes in handy.

Once you know that this first sheet of paneling is perfectly straight, nail down both sides of the panel every twelve inches. This secures the sheet.

You have placed the studs sixteen inches apart on center. This means you will have two studs behind every panel that is four feet in width.

Put a few nails through the paneling into the studs behind it. Be sure to use a nail set so the hammer will not damage the finish of the paneling. You can get by with one nail at the top, which will be covered by the cove molding, one in the middle, which you may wish to touch up so it does not show, and one at the bottom, which is covered by the baseboard. The vertical edges of each sheet must be fastened to studs with nails twelve inches apart.

Now, continue along the wall, nailing the panels exactly as you did the first piece. Make periodic checks with the level to make sure the panels are still straight.

When you come to the end of a wall, you will probably have to cut the last sheet to a different width. This cut is done in the same manner as you cut the top of each panel. Just remember to measure the width you need and to take your time in cutting to avoid any ripping or tearing.

Where there are electrical outlets, you will need to cut the panels so the outlets show through. This is done with a keyhole saw. Lean the panel against the wall, but do not nail it in place. Make a rough mark on the face of the wood where the outlet will be. Lay the panel across the two supports. Measure accurately the horizontal distance from the edge of the last sheet to the outlet. Then measure from the ceiling (or the floor, if it is closer) to the outlet (see Illustration 58). Go back to the panel and, using a ruler, mark the correct opening on the panel face. This should line up with the rough mark you made when the panel was against the wall. If not, recheck your measurements, for once you cut a piece out of a panel, you cannot replace it.

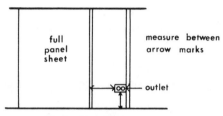

full
panel
sheet

measure between
arrow marks

outlet

Illustration 58

Drill a hole in the center of the area to be cut so that you have a place to insert the keyhole saw. Start in the center; then, should the wood splinter, only the part that will be removed will be damaged. Pull the saw toward one corner of the square you have marked on the wood. Rather than trying to make a right angle turn (which could split the wood), make another cut from the center to the same side, but over about one inch. Remove this chip, and you have an open area in which to continue the cutting. It really doesn't matter if the edges are a little bit ragged as long as the hole is not too large. The cover plate that goes over the outlet will cover the edges of the hole (see Illustration 59).

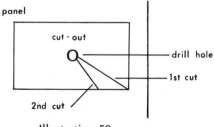

panel

cut - out

drill hole

1st cut

2nd cut

Illustration 59

If you purchased unfinished moldings, stain them to

match the paneling before you attach them to the wall. It is much easier to paint a separate piece of wood than it is to paint the molding when it is in place. Then neatness really counts—and that takes time.

The baseboard is put on first along the bottom edge of the paneling. Use finishing nails (nails without heads), and countersink them by using the nail set and hammer. On top of this piece, directly along the floor line, goes the base shoe or quarter round. Purchase an inexpensive miter box so that you can cut the end pieces on the correct angle for a perfect fit.

The ceiling molding (cove) goes on the paneling with its top edge fitted tightly to the ceiling. However, if you intend to install a new ceiling, do not put this piece up until you have done so. The nails go through the paneling, not the ceiling. Should you find that the nail holes are visible, fill them in with wood putty, sand smooth, and stain them so they will not show.

In the corners use inside corner molding. This will conceal the rough-cut edges. Corner molding is inserted between the cove and the baseboard. This is explained further in the directions for installing mirrored wall tiles.

If you have doors in your room, you need a carpenter. Doors are too tricky for an amateur to install. After the doors are hung, you will put molding around the three sides of the door frame. Put the cover plates back on the outlets and you're done!

Building a bar isn't ordinarily a do-it-yourself project for a woman, or for that matter, for a man. You must be adept at using a saw and be able to handle large and heavy pieces of plywood. Some people purchase preassembled bars and just fasten them in place. Let me express one thought on the preassembled, or portable, bar. If you do buy one, be sure to anchor it securely to the floor. A few years ago our neighbors, who had a free-standing portable bar, had company and, while the adults were visiting, a three-year-old child tried to climb up the bar. It fell on top of her, and she was seriously injured. So, if you do choose a portable bar, fasten it securely to the floor.

I figure, however, if you can stud out a room and hang paneling, then constructing a bar should not be impossible for you. But before you start, read all the instructions and be very sure that you can do the job. If not, hire a carpenter. You've already saved so much money that you can afford to spend some on hired labor.

There are many different ways of building a bar—probably as many ways as there are handymen. Some say build a frame out of two-by-fours and cross-brace it from behind. Others suggest building the entire unit and then bolting it to the floor. Your local lumber dealer will probably have a totally different approach and a professional carpenter yet another method. I am going to give you one way that isn't too difficult.

First, you must determine where you want the bar, although this should already have been done when you were deciding whether or not you needed extra electrical outlets. Second, decide how long you want the bar to be and whether you want it straight or "L" shaped. I am not going into a curved bar because it is entirely too difficult for an amateur. Keep in mind that you will probably want a back bar (against the paneled wall) for storing liquor, glasses, dishes, a hot plate, and other items.

When laying out the bar area, remember that the back bar will stand out from the wall approximately sixteen inches, and you will need walking and working room between it and the front bar. An area four feet wide should suffice, although a little less is permissible. Don't skimp on the space between the two bars. When you are entertaining a small group of people, you may find that one or two people prefer sitting behind the bar while the others sit in front. While only you can decide on the shape and placement of your bar, I'll present one idea for a layout which happens to be the one I used (see Illustration 60).

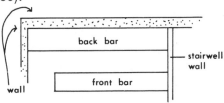

Illustration 60

A bar is usually forty-two inches high, with a nine-inch-deep ledge for a footrest (you can eliminate this if you like). The ledge is elevated nine inches from the floor.

The basic frame of the bar is made of three-quarter-inch plywood. One four-foot-by-eight-foot sheet will make four framing pieces (also called uprights). You need a framing piece at each end of the bar and several more between the ends. If you are constructing a six-foot-long bar, you will need one sheet of plywood for the uprights.

Illustration 61 shows the spacing of the uprights for a six-foot-long bar, as viewed from the front of the bar. Mark the positions of the uprights as follows: Draw the outline of the base of the bar on the floor where the bar will stand. Measure carefully, for the lines you draw will be the guidelines for constructing the bar. Use chalk to draw the lines so that you can make changes easily. Next, starting at one end of the bar, make chalk marks at two-foot intervals along the front and the back of the bar. (If the bar were six feet long, you would mark off three two-foot intervals.) Connect the marks from front to back. These lines guide the placement of the framing pieces.

The framing pieces that serve as the ends of the bar are positioned so that the outside edge is on the guideline. The other (interior) framing pieces are positioned so that the plywood piece is centered on the guidelines.

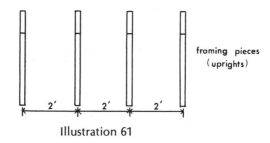

Illustration 61

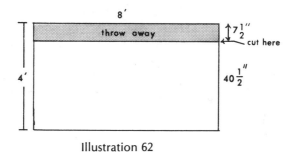

Illustration 62

Place the sheet of plywood on the floor so the eight-foot side is facing you. Measure seven and one-half inches up from the long edge and draw a line across the board (see Illustration 62). This piece can be cut off and thrown away, now or later. Follow Illustration 62 to draw the cutting lines for the first upright. Illustration 63 shows how to measure and draw the lines for the rest of the uprights.

You will need some two-by-fours to construct the

base of each framing piece, one twenty-four-inch two-
by-four for each upright. (I assume that you have on

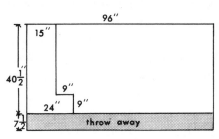

Illustration 63

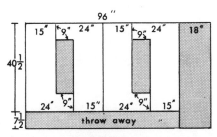

Illustration 64

hand enough prefinished paneling, left over from your
wall paneling project, to finish the entire unit. If you
don't, you will have to measure the area to be covered
and buy the paneling.)

Once you have drawn lines on the floor to guide the
construction of the bar, and drawn the cutting lines on
the sheet of plywood, it is time to cut out the uprights.
Do the cutting with a power saw (but be sure to wear
safety glasses). First, cut off the seven-and-a-half-inch
strip along the long side of the board, if you have not
already done so.

Cut the framing pieces, following the lines you drew
on the plywood. Next, nail each framing piece to the

two-inch side of a two-by-four, making sure that the edge of the two-by-four and the edge of the upright are aligned (see Illustration 65). Use eight-penny nails. It doesn't matter which side of the upright you nail the two-by-four to—except on the uprights that serve as the ends of the bar. The two-by-fours that support these uprights must be attached to the side of the upright that is inside the bar.

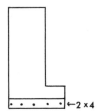

Illustration 65

Now, set one framing piece at one end of the bar area, making sure that the two-by-four is inside the bar and the outside edge of the plywood is on the guideline. Nail the two-by-four to the floor. (Refer to Illustration 53 and the instructions for using the Fas-N-It for nailing into concrete.) Raise the next upright, center it on the guideline, and nail it to the floor. Continue down the line until you have all the framing pieces raised and nailed in place.

Remember that the two-by-four of the end framing piece must be inside the bar area—not outside. Also, if your bar is longer or shorter than six feet, as in our example, the distance between the last framing piece and the one next to it may be less than two feet. Don't worry about it—that's the way the ball bounces.

Now construct the base for the top of the bar. Again,

you will use sheets of three-quarter-inch plywood. You have already determined that the bar top will be fifteen inches from the back to where it meets the front paneling. Add nine inches to this measurement (making a twenty-four-inch-wide bar top). This is the section that overhangs the front of the bar so that you have knee room and can still rest your elbows on the top while "swigging that beer."

Cut a four-by-eight-foot piece of plywood in half the long way (see Illustration 66) and you will have two twenty-four-inch-wide top pieces. Trim them to the overall length of the bar top. Nail one of the trimmed pieces to the tops of the framing pieces.

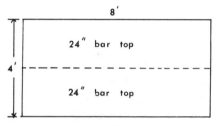

Illustration 66

Place the second board on top of the first and nail it down. This gives you a one-and-a-half-inch-thick plywood bar-top base and raises the entire bar height to the recommended forty-two inches. Construct the top of the footrest in the same way, except that the board will be nine inches in width and you will need only one layer of the three-quarter-inch plywood.

You may wish to have shelves in the front bar. If you do, nail shelf holders of two-by-two-inch pieces of lumber along the width of each framing piece. On top of these lay half-inch or three-quarter-inch plywood and nail it in place (see Illustration 67).

Very little is left to do. Cut the paneling to fit the framing of the bar and nail it to the uprights. Follow the

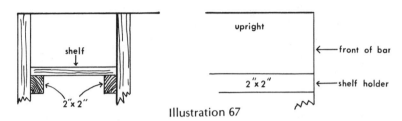

Illustration 67

directions for cutting and installing paneling for walls. Panel the front and sides of the bar, including the front of the footrest. Use finishing nails, countersink them, and fill the holes if they show.

The next decision to make is how to finish the bar top and the footrest. You could use mosaic tile (my favorite). Or you could use shellacked, water-resistant wood, or Formica, or a leather-look covering. Choose whatever appeals to you, cut it to size, and apply according to the directions that come with the material.

All that is left is to cover up the rough edges. For the edges of the top of the bar, there is a special piece of wood called "bar nosing" which is sold in lumber stores. It is curved to cover the edge and to extend onto the bar top. Bar nosing can be as plain or as ornate as you wish.

Purchase outside corner molding and nail it in place where the paneling meets at right angles. Where the footrest meets the paneling of the bar, attach a piece of inside corner molding. On the outer edges of the footrest, you can use either outside molding or a piece of metal stripping (the outside-angle type). I prefer to use metal here as people have a tendency to scrape their feet along this edge, and this wears down and mars the wood.

The back bar is built in the same way as the front (but without the footrest), except that you will need a carpenter to cut and hang the doors if you want them. You could hang curtains (café-type) which slide open easily. Or you could use the plastic "bamboo" type curtains. Here again, your taste and budget dictate.

Ceilings and Stair Treatment

I have chosen to put ceiling and stair treatment in a separate chapter rather than include them in the chapter on finishing the basement. One obvious reason is that that chapter was getting too long. But more important is the fact that you may wish to redo ceilings other than the basement ceiling. Should your house be quite old, the high ceilings may not be to your liking. A high ceiling can be beautiful, but it can also be an eyesore, depending upon its treatment. Dropping a high ceiling to an eight-foot height can help you conserve quite a bit of heating fuel, too.

Perhaps water has leaked through a ceiling. This can occur when some dumb person doesn't shut the shower doors completely or neglects to put the shower curtain (which I hope you replaced with sliding doors) inside the tub. However, a stopped-up outside gutter or a loose roof shingle can also result in water damage to your ceiling. You can, of course, call in a plasterer to repair the ceiling. Hopefully, your insurance will cover it. But maybe you never liked that old ceiling anyway. So why not replace it?

You may wish to change a perfectly good ceiling to match the decor of the room. Let's say you want your family room to take on a rustic look. What better way than to install fake wood beams! I have a friend who purchased a brand-new house. The family room was attractive, but not outstanding. Her husband (she hadn't read this book!) put fake beams on the ceiling. The difference was remarkable. The family room adjoined the kitchen, so he put the beams in both rooms. For an expenditure of a few dollars, the rooms were totally transformed.

Fake beams are made of plastic. When installed, they look as if they weigh a ton, but in reality are so light that one person can put them up. They are glued onto the ceiling with a special adhesive sold with them. All that you have to do first is to draw straight lines across the ceiling to guide your placement of the beams. Spread the mastic on the beam and press it onto the ceiling, making sure to follow the straight line you have drawn.

Don't overlook the fact that ceiling tile can be used in any room in the house. There is special tile with a plastic coating for the kitchen. The coating makes the tile as easy to wash as a painted ceiling. There is moisture-proof tile for use in a bathroom or laundry room, where excessive dampness is a problem.

We tend to associate acoustical tile with a basement, but that is not the only place it's useful. If your children have a stereo set in their bedroom, try acoustical tile on the ceiling. I won't guarantee that the room will be soundproof, but you'll be able to rest in your own room without ear plugs.

To explain what acoustical tile is takes no more than a few sentences. It is ceiling tile, with small holes in it, that absorbs sound. This does not mean it totally obliterates noise, but it does deaden it considerably. The lower the ceiling of a room, the higher the potential noise level. The American Medical Association is constantly preaching that we are slowly losing our hearing due to noise pollution. Any steps we can take to correct this will enhance our own health and the health of our children (even though they won't appreciate it now).

It used to be that all ceiling tile looked alike—plain white squares. When you visit your home remodeling center, you will be amazed at the wide variety of tile offered today. Although white is still the most popular, you can also purchase ceiling tile in sea green, pale blue, and other shades. A favorite of mine is white with gold flecks. This tile can be as formal or informal as one likes. Some tile has a random pattern, such as green fern fronds, running through each piece.

The old twelve-by-twelve-inch size has also been updated. Not that the twelve-inch square piece is not used—on the contrary, it still is the most popular size sold. But consider one alternative—tile that, when installed, looks like wood boards. It comes in varying widths and lengths. The finish so resembles wood that only a pro would know it wasn't the real thing.

You will find, when shopping for ceiling tile, that the price of a certain tile will vary considerably from store to store. Look around. You will probably find a store that sells what you want at a reduced cost. Be sure to watch sale advertisements, too. But be positive that when you price shop you compare identical tile made by the same manufacturer. Check the pattern run, number, and series just as you did with wallpaper and floor tile.

Because ceiling tile varies greatly in price, it is vital

that you know why this occurs and the differences in the products offered. Otherwise you might purchase tile that is not suited to your purpose.

The most reasonably priced tile is the plain white twelve-inch square type. There is absolutely nothing wrong with this tile if it suits you. I have seen white tile on sale for as little as nine cents apiece.

As the quality of the material increases, the cost increases. Let's consider the types of tile available. Each type listed costs more than the previous one; you alone can decide what you want and need.

After the standard white comes acoustical (sound-absorbing) tile. As I mentioned previously, acoustical tile is great for a basement, a family room, or a child's bedroom, where you definitely want less noise.

Next in line is embossed tile. This tile has a wavy look and is not the same thickness throughout. Embossed tile resembles a brocaded fabric. The only drawback, as far as I'm concerned, is that it is difficult to clean. Then we come to washable tile. This does cost more, but it's worth it if you are going to use the tile in a kitchen where frequent washing is necessary.

Fifth in line is colored tile. Naturally it will cost more because it takes more of the manufacturer's time to prepare. The demand also is not great. There are many rooms where you might want colored tile to go with the existing color scheme or where you want the ceiling to be noticed.

There also is tile that has a sculptured look. The finished ceiling has no visible seams; the installed tile has the appearance of being one continuous sheet. It is commonly used in a foyer, living room, or dining room, where the lack of seams is the deciding factor in the choice of a ceiling material.

Vinyl-surface tile ranks next on the cost index. I would not hesitate to recommend this for a kitchen—above and beyond the "washable" tile. As we homemakers know, the least amount of housework we have to do is the best! So, spend a few more dollars for vinyl tile, and in the long run you will be repaid with labor saved.

One of the most expensive kinds of ceiling tile is fireproof tile. Under normal circumstances this kind of tile is used only in offices, restaurants, and buildings that must meet a fire code. It might be a good idea to install fireproof tile in a basement that has only one exit. However, you must consider that most fires do not start in the ceiling. A carelessly discarded cigarette that drops into a couch is a more common cause. Smoke inhalation kills many more people than fire does. My suggestion is that, unless you are really concerned about fire, you forget about fireproof tile.

There is one other type of ceiling tile you may want to consider. This is the "luminous" panel that is installed below a long fluorescent bulb. The light comes through the tile and is diffused over the entire panel to create a low and even lighting tone. The light fixtures are installed first and then the grids and panels. I'll cover this in the different ways of installing tile ceilings. However, if you are tiling a basement ceiling that is only seven feet high to begin with, you surely would not wish to drop the ceiling any further. To do so would cause the room to "close in."

Now that I have covered the different types of tile available, it is time to deal with installation. How you put tile up depends upon the room.

I assume that you have read the preceding chapters and know, therefore, how to determine the quantity of tile you will need. If you are interested only in putting up a ceiling and have skipped the previous chapters, this information is given here in capsule form.

Measure the length and then the width of the ceiling. Multiply one measurement by the other.

For example, if the room measures twenty feet by fifteen feet, multiply the length (twenty feet) by the width (fifteen feet). You would require three hundred square feet of tile. If the tiles are twelve inches square, you need three hundred pieces. Probably the ceiling of your room cannot be evenly divided into twelve-inch squares. In that case you need extra tile that you can cut to fit around the edges of the ceiling. As I have stated before, always purchase a little more material than you actually need. You never know when replacement may be necessary, and too, you will probably break a few tiles while installing them.

Let's begin with the easiest installation first: tiling over an existing finished ceiling. The fact that a ceiling is already present does not mean that the surface is exactly square. A plaster ceiling can be off center by several inches, and who can tell? But tile, with the exception of sculptured tile that has no visible seams, must be centered on the ceiling, or the end cuts will be uneven. However, even with the sculptured tile, you will not want to end up with a one-inch wide strip along one edge of the ceiling. Try to arrange the tile so that any necessary cuts are even on either side. If you are using sculptured tile, you may be able to use a full tile along one wall and a half tile on the opposite side. This saves tile and cutting time. But you cannot do this when there are visible seams.

The starting point for laying floor tile is in the center of the room. This is not the case when installing ceiling tile. Because ceiling tile has tongue-and groove edges, you must start in one corner of the room and work outward from this point. The reason for this is simple: when you staple (or cement, as the case may be) one tile into place, the next one must fit into it in such a way that it covers the recessed piece.

When you purchase your tile, the manufacturer, or dealer, will supply you with a sheet outlining the way to install that particular tile. Read these instructions carefully and follow them. Otherwise, should anything go wrong, your warranty will be void. However, some of these instruction sheets are so sparse that it is hard to understand them unless you have some background. So, I'll present my way with simple-to-understand illustrations and hope that this will make the manufacturer's instructions clearer.

Since we are primarily concerned with a basement ceiling, I'll just touch lightly on putting tile on an existing ceiling (that is, one that is already installed, as in a kitchen or den, and does not have any exposed joists). It is possible to install tile over an existing ceiling with an adhesive. You cannot use an adhesive if the existing ceiling is wallboard nailed to joists that are more than sixteen inches apart. Nor can you use adhesive on a ceiling that has wallpaper or many coats of old and chipped paint on it, or if the ceiling is plaster and is cracked or has an uneven surface. In other words, the existing ceiling must be in perfect shape before you can use an adhesive. If the ceiling has one or more of these problems, you will have to fur the ceiling.

Now for a few definitions before we begin. Joists are the parallel beams that extend from wall to wall and hold up the floor or ceiling. They are usually sixteen inches apart on center (the center of one joist is sixteen inches from the center of the next).

Should you need to locate a joist in an existing ceiling, there are many different ways of doing so. Some people recommend knocking on the ceiling until you do not hear a "hollow" sound. A hollow sound means there is no joist in that part of the ceiling. A solid sound when you rap means you have found the joist. Very hard on the knuckles!

Others say drill a few holes in the ceiling and see if the drill goes through or hits the joist. Very messy! The easiest way is to go to the hardware store and purchase a "stud finder." This tool is inexpensive and efficient. By its very name you know you can use it on walls if you need to locate studs. The stud finder has a magnetized needle that moves when passed over a nail. That nail is holding up the joist. Make a mark on the ceiling over the nail and you know where the first joist is. Measure out sixteen inches and use the stud finder again. If the needle moves, you know the joists are the correct sixteen inches apart, on center.

Now we come to furring strips. These will be needed for a basement ceiling and for an existing ceiling that does not meet the rigid requirements for adhesive application. Professionals may use one-by-two-inch strips. Don't try it! They are very narrow, and if you are not perfect (and who is?), you will miss the strips after a number of tiles have been put up. Instead, use one-by-three-inch softwood furring pieces. They allow for a little mistake now and then—but not a big one!

Now you must determine the layout of the ceiling tile. Try to keep the border along one wall the same width as the border along the facing (opposite) wall. Otherwise you throw off the balance of the room.

I am going to quote Armstrong Cork Company's directions for figuring the width of the border tiles. They are accurate and easy to understand. I have added a few extra words, but the basic instructions are Armstrong's. These directions assume that you are using twelve-by-twelve-inch tile and that the room is not exactly divisible by one square foot.

Let's begin by figuring the border tile for the long wall. It sounds funny, but the measurement is made on the short wall.

1. Measure one of the short walls in the room.
2. If this measurement is not an exact number of feet, add twelve inches to the inches left over.
3. Divide the total number of inches by two. This will give you the width of the border tile for the long wall.

EXAMPLE:

1. Short wall		is	10′ 8″
2. Extra inches		are	8″
3. Add			12″
4. Divide	2 into		20″
5. Border tile for long wall is			10″

Border tile for the short walls is figured using the same procedure, except you measure the long wall.

EXAMPLE:

1. Long wall		is	12′4″
2. Extra inches		are	4″
3. Add			12″
4. Divide	2 into		16″
5. Border tile for short wall is			8″

It is vital that you make this determination before you begin nailing up the furring strips. If the strips are not correctly placed, you will have nothing on which to staple the tiles.

The first (and last) furring strip is nailed flush against the wall at right angles to the joists (in other words, across the joists). Lay it against the wall and up tight to the joists. Nail the strip in place at the first joist location using two eight-penny nails. Place your carpenter's square where the strip and the joist meet. Move the furring strip so that there is a tight fit on both sides of the square. Nail this section in. Continue down the line, using the carpenter's square at each juncture, until the first furring strip is secured to the overhead joists.

The second furring strip is now placed parallel to the first strip. The distance between the centers of the furring strips should be the width of the border tile. In the example given, the border tile width for the long wall was ten inches. Add one-half inch for the flange. The second furring strip should be placed so that the center is ten and one-half inches from the center of the first furring strip. You have now completed the most difficult steps in furring out the ceiling.

Use your level to make sure that the furring pieces are projecting straight down from the joists (see Illustration 68). If not, it may be necessary to insert wood shims between the strips and the joists. Shims are small, thin pieces of wood that any lumberyard will be glad to give you. If the furring strips are very uneven, return them for new ones. If they are just a little uneven, you can straighten them by inserting shims.

Continue across the joists, nailing the rest of the furring strips in place twelve inches apart, on center.

Remember, twelve inches on center does not mean twelve inches between each two furring strips. Rather, it

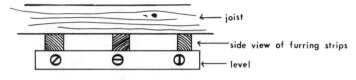

Illustration 68

means twelve inches from the middle of one piece to the middle of the next.

You have already determined the width of the border tile; the next to the last furring strip should be that number of inches away from the wall minus the one-half inch you added on to the measurement for the first strip. In the example given, the distance from the wall would be nine and one-half inches. You put the last furring strip against the wall, just as you did the first.

Sometimes you will have pipes or ducts that extend down below the joists. Or, you may wish to put tile under the "I" beam. You will have to box these in with furring strips (see Illustration 69). Just remember to keep these strips in line with the ones on the ceiling, or the order of the tile will be thrown off.

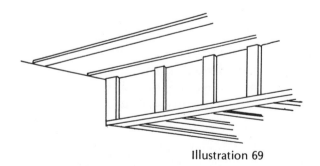

Illustration 69

Once the furring strips are in place, you must determine your starting point for the tile. As I mentioned before, you start in one corner of the room—not in the dead center as you would for a floor. You need two reference lines to align the first rows of tile in both directions or the border tiles will not fit properly.

Refer to Illustration 70 while reading these instructions. You will need a chalk line and a tape measure. To make the first line, snap your chalk line dead center down the center of the second furring strip from the wall.

Next you are going to make a chalk line across the furring strips at a distance from the wall equal to the width of the border tile on the short wall. In the example, this measurement is eight and one-half inches. Measure out from the wall that distance on five studs, including the first and the last. Snap the chalk line over these marks. The point where the two chalk lines cross is point A.

In order to get a perfect right angle (where you will place that first, and most important, tile), it is necessary to make three more measurements: 1. From point A, measure down the furring strip exactly three feet. Mark this point B. 2. Go back to A and, using the chalk line you have made as a guide, measure across the joists exactly four feet. Mark this point C. 3. Connect B and C by use of the chalk line. Measure the distance from B to C. It must be exactly five feet.

If the line that connects B to C is not exactly five feet, make a slight adjustment in the line A-C. But recheck all your measurements before changing A-C so that you get a B-C length of five feet.

Now to begin the installation of the tile. Measure and cut the border tiles individually. When measuring a

tile to be cut, include the flange piece in the measurement. (The flange is the flat, recessed piece that you put

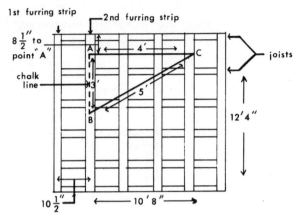

Illustration 70

the staples in.) In the example given, the corner tile
would be eight and one-half by ten and one-half inches.
The extra one-half inch is the measurement of the
flange. Align this tile with the two flange sides along lines
A-C and A-B which you have extended to the walls (see
Illustration 71). Staple the tile into place, using a staple
gun that you can rent or buy and nine-sixteenths-inch
staples. Insert three staples along the flange edge that is
on the furring strip and one staple in the furring strip
next to the wall.

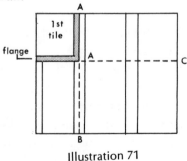

Illustration 71

Cut the second tile so that one of the tongue edges fits into the corner tile and the stapling flange falls directly on line A-B. Staple it into place as you did the first piece. Cut the third tile so that the tongue edge fits into the corner tile and the flange falls directly on line A-C (see Illustration 72).

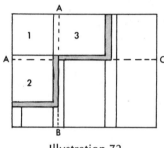

Illustration 72

Continue cutting and attaching two or three more border tiles, lining them up along A-C on the short wall and A-B on the long wall. Fill in the space between with whole tiles, inserting one tile into the groove in the adjoining tile and stapling it to the furring strips. Stop every now and then to check your progress. You can always rip one or two tiles out, but who can afford to remove an entire ceiling?

Continue across and down the room until you come to the other two border walls. They are completed exactly as you did the first two. Cove molding, or ceiling molding, is then installed to cover the seam where the cut tiles meet the walls.

A suspended ceiling (one that hangs below an existing ceiling or from joists) requires measuring to determine border tile size and starting point. The procedure is the same as that for regular tile. Since each manufacturer sells special hanging equipment, it would be foolish for me to go into any one way to put up a suspended ceiling. Suffice it to say that such a ceiling is made up of a simple metal framework (called the grid) that is suspended from the ceiling on wires. The ceiling panels are then dropped down into the grid.

Grids come in a variety of colors, and the tiles are usually two feet square or two feet by four feet. If you choose a suspended ceiling, follow the manufacturer's directions to the letter. Such a ceiling is not difficult to install. You can put a light above one or more panels (between the suspended panels and the existing ceiling) and install a "luminous" panel.

If you choose to install tiles that look like wood paneling, you will find they are longer and narrower than the average tile. The directions for installing this kind of tile are the same as for square tile, except that you will need more furring strips because of the reduced width of the tile and more staples down the length of the tile. Always make accurate measurements before installing the furring strips for this type of ceiling tile.

Another idea for redoing a ceiling is the use of stucco-type paint. It can be sprayed on, but I certainly wouldn't suggest doing this in a room that has furniture that can't be moved or in one that has carpeting. Ask your paint dealer to show you stucco paint (not paint *for* stucco). You can apply it easily and its rough, uneven finish is fascinating on a ceiling, especially if you combine it with fake beams.

That takes care of just about every major area you could improve in a house, with the exception of stairs.

Stair covering may not seem important, but your treatment of stairs can easily "make or break" the decor of a room. Who wants to enter a beautifully finished basement by going down old wooden steps? By the same token, if you have installed a new foyer in a two-story house, do you want to look at worn carpeting on the stairs to the second floor?

I don't suggest that you attempt to fully cover each step. This entails exact cutting and fitting. You would have to turn under the sides and secure them on each step, not a job for a beginner. Since the carpeting would have to be ordered to size, it wouldn't cost too much more to have it installed professionally.

Instead, purchase what is called a stair runner. This is a piece of carpeting already cut in a strip, with the edges finished. I think a little bit of wood on either side of carpeting gives a nice contrast. However, if the wood is unfinished or in bad condition, stain it before you put down the runner.

Stair runners come in almost any carpeting material. I used indoor-outdoor carpeting on the basement stairs. That was eight years ago, and it still looks perfect despite constant traffic. It is easy to clean, but, best of all, rarely needs it. You can purchase a runner in plush, tweed, or just about any pattern that appeals to you.

As you consider stair treatment, allow me to put in a few negatives. First, *never* use ceramic tile on stairs. There are three reasons for this, two of which could literally kill you. Let's cover the nonlethal one first. Because stairs are narrow in both length and width, they have a tendency to expand and contract. Also, all the weight of a person is centered on the step, making it "give" a little. This expanding, contracting, and bending can cause the ceramic tile to chip, crack, or loosen.

The second reason is even more important. Ceramic tile is slippery, and if there is one place you don't want to fall, it is down the stairs.

Third, if you were to install ceramic tile on stairs you

would have to put a steel nosing (strip) along the edge of each stair. It would be all too easy to hook your toe on it and pitch forward. This is one reason why I never recommend resilient floor tile on stairs. The nosing strip is necessary with this type of tile also. Because the strip sticks up above the tile, it presents a real hazard, especially if you have small children or are wearing high heels. So, stick to carpeting—it's safer!

For our purposes, all we need to know about stair construction is that each stair is made up of two parts. First is the tread, or the part we walk on. The second is called the riser, the vertical piece that holds up the tread (see Illustration 73).

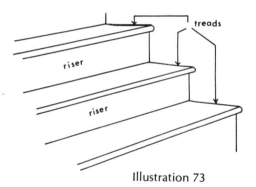

Illustration 73

It's no problem to decide how much carpeting you will need. Runners are sold by the running foot or yard, not in square yards as is regular carpeting. Measure in inches the height of the riser and the depth of the tread. Add these two measurements together and multiply this figure by the number of stairs. Since you are working in inches, you will need to divide the total by twelve to get the correct number of running feet or by thirty-six to obtain running yards. Purchase at least one-half yard more than you actually need.

You may wish to use padding under the runner. I didn't on the basement steps, and I can't see that this made any difference. However, you may like the thick look that padding gives. If you are going to pad, purchase individual pads. They are easier (and cheaper) to work with than one long continuous sheet of padding. You don't need padding on the riser anyway. Purchase pads that are about one inch narrower in width than the runner. This way the padding will not show at the edges of the runner. Also, make sure that the pads are deep enough to cover the entire tread and overlap at the edge. Ordinary tacks hold them in place at the back of the tread and again under the front edge (nose).

There are many different ways to install a runner. One is with tacks, but they do show. Another way is with staples. This is what I used on the basement runner. Use a staple gun, and insert the staples directly in the crease where the tread meets the riser and again underneath the nose of the tread. The staples are barely visible.

You can also use double-faced adhesive tape. This must be purchased from a carpet dealer, as it is a special kind of tape. Put one strip of tape at the bottom of the riser, another at the back of the tread, and a third on the front of the tread around the nose.

You can also use tackless strips that are commonly used in wall-to-wall carpet installation. Nail them down at the back of the tread where the riser and tread meet. The small hooks on the strip hold the carpeting in place. Another method is to use carpet rods. Put two eye screws, one on each side of the step, into the riser where it meets the tread. Then, after setting the runner in place, insert the rod over the carpet and through the eye screws. I don't like carpet rods, but you might like them, so check them out.

The tackless strips are, of course, nailed in before you lay the carpeting. If you have padding, this, too, is tacked down first. Double-faced adhesive tape is also put down first. Regardless of the method you choose, always begin at the top of the stairs. Stand at the head of the stairs and let the runner unfold down the entire stairway. Make sure you have it centered on the stairs (that is, an equal amount of wood shows on both sides of the runner).

Tack the runner to the edge of the top riser (see Illustration 74). Now secure the runner at the place where the tread and riser meet by whichever method you chose. Continue down each step, checking to see that the runner is straight and attaching the carpet at the tread and riser junction.

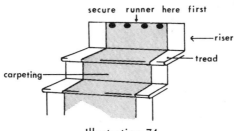

Illustration 74

Do not cut off the excess at the bottom—turn it under. Tack it down at the bottom of the last riser. Then, if the carpeting begins to show wear, you can loosen it, unfold the excess piece, and move the entire runner up the stairs. This way the worn areas (usually on the nose edge) are laid flat on the tread and will not be so noticeable.

Finishing Touches and Other Ideas

    If you have accomplished everything that has been set forth in these chapters, you qualify as a champion home remodeler. The house you have now is not the house you started with, for now it is totally yours. You have used your ideas and labor, and can take pride in a job well done.

    You may ask yourself what more you can possibly do in the area of decorating and remodeling. This chapter will cover a variety of ideas you may wish to try or to adapt to fit your particular needs.

    When you visit your local home improvement center, you will be startled by the variety of different materials you can utilize to transform a room. Just to mention a few: fake fireplaces that look like the real thing; glass mirror tiles that you can install in one afternoon; fake brick that looks (and feels) like the real thing; and imitation cork wall covering that does not require the upkeep of real cork.

Consider divider posts that, when installed, appear to support the ceiling, and murals that are painted by number and are as pretty as any painted by a professional artist. There are glass-block windows that you can install in either a bathroom or a basement. How about building a brick patio? Glass bookshelves make a welcomed addition to any room. Instead of drapes, you may want louvered shutters. They lend themselves beautifully to a colonial decor. Don't forget the many uses of pegboard in a garage, an attic, or a basement. This list covers only some of the many ideas open to you.

Let's start this chapter with the use of a fake fireplace. It used to be that "fake" was a dirty word to anyone who loved the warm glow of a fireplace. This is no longer true. Many of us have purchased houses without fireplaces and want to have one in the den, the basement, the living room, or even in a bedroom. The cost of having a real one installed is astronomical. Consider the expense of making an opening in the roof for a chimney, not to mention cutting through the wall for the duct or making the wall opening. However, to me, these are not the major drawbacks to the real thing. I hate the soot that gathers, cleaning out the ashes, trying to start the fire with newspaper, and the discoloration of the surrounding brick.

Take a look at the fake fireplaces available today. They are beautiful. You can choose a wall-hung unit, which can be traditional, colonial, or contemporary in design. Other types sit directly on the floor and have a mantel on top. There is even a copy of the old Ben Franklin stove. You can recess the floor-standing models into the wall, but this entails either cutting into the existing wall or building a new wall out around the fireplace. Cutting into the wall is a major project, and extending the existing wall cuts down on the room size.

There is nothing to the installation of a fake fireplace. The logs in some are illuminated by a light bulb. All you need is an electrical outlet nearby. Some of the more expensive models are gas operated. Installation entails having a plumbing contractor come in to attach a gas pipeline. This procedure is mentioned on the assumption that you already have a gas line into your home. Even so, the cost will be high. If you have an all-electric home, forget it.

Wall-hung units are simple to install. They are either nailed or screwed to the studs in the wall. Since each unit has its own screw fastenings, you must follow the manufacturer's directions for hanging. However, before you install the unit, be sure there is an electrical outlet handy if the fireplace requires one. If there isn't, you will need an electrical contractor to install one. Remember, don't fool around with electricity—it's much too dangerous for an amateur.

A free-standing unit is easier to place. Just put it against the wall and plug it in. Lights that revolve under the logs make it look like the real thing. These units may be a little more expensive than wall-hung units, but they are worth it. There is no danger of fire, but the illusion is that of a real fireplace.

There is one great advantage to the electric fireplace: it is completely portable. You can move it from room to room or take it with you when you move. If you are lucky enough to own a summer house, you can use your electric fireplace there during the season and then take it home for the winter. Some electric fireplaces even have a built-in heating unit that makes them not only beautiful but also functional.

Have you looked at the glass mirror tile now available? A few years ago, I used them in my living room, and I was limited by the small selection available. In those days you could get only plain mirror glass, or glass with gold or black veins.

Today you can get mirror tile with pictures of ships, scenic views, or figures. Not that I suggest doing an entire wall with scenes or ships. That would be absolutely overwhelming. If you decide to use picture tile, surround one picture with eight plain or veined tiles (see Illustration 75).

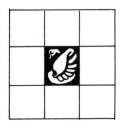

Illustration 75

Installing mirror tiles is a simple operation when done correctly. Unfortunately, my first attempt was a fiasco which I will describe even though it makes me look like less of an authority than I'd like to appear.

My husband and I decided we'd like mirror tile in our living room. We felt it would make the room look larger (which it certainly does) and we wanted to create a focal point behind our stereo console. The wall was eighty-four inches wide, which meant we would have seven vertical rows of tile. Like most living rooms, ours is seven feet in height, so the job entailed no cutting of tiles.

Back to my mistake. Having never previously put mirror tile on a wall, and neglecting to obtain any instructions, I really goofed! But how do we learn except by our mistakes or those of someone else? So you profit by mine.

I assumed that mirror tile was installed the same way

as floor tile—that is, starting in the middle of the wall at a center line. Please look at Illustration 76 but *do not* follow it. Doing so courts disaster.

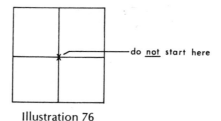

—do <u>not</u> start here

Illustration 76

To make a long story short, I drew a horizontal line across the wall and then made the vertical line. I took great pains with the measurements to be certain I did not have to cut the glass. But there was one thing I didn't figure on. The tile slid down the wall—and I mean slid! I didn't realize that the weight of the tile would make this inevitable. Since I had started in the center of the wall, it was impossible to prevent the tile from sliding. When it was time to install the next row, the first row had moved down the wall past the center line, and my level line was concealed by the slipping tiles.

Unfortunately, two neighbors (both men!) were present and witnessed the mess. So we all make mistakes, but who needs onlookers?

I put up paneling on either side of the mirror tile, because I have a collection of Royal Doulton figurines, which, I felt, could be effectively displayed on small shelves set on paneling. These shelves are staggered in order to show off each figure to its best advantage (see Illustration 77). Maybe you have a collection you wish to display. Why not show it off properly?

To affix mirror tile to the wall you will need to remove the base shoe or quarter round and the baseboard for the length of the wall you are going to mirror. Although removing the baseboard will damage the wall, you can fill in any holes with spackle, and the

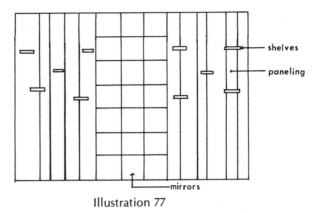

Illustration 77

tile will cover it. Also remove the ceiling molding. Check Chapter 2 (Laying Ceramic Tile) for ways to remove these pieces without breaking them. Set them aside, for you will need to replace them when you are finished tiling.

Mirror tiles, as I learned from sad experience, are applied from the bottom of the wall upwards. It is imperative that you have something to support that first row of tile as the adhesive dries. As I stated before, a line on the wall will not suffice.

Hopefully, you will not need to cut any of the tiles. However, if you do, make your cuts on the bottom row rather than the top. An ordinary glass cutter will cut the mirrors. A glass cutter can be purchased at any hardware store. It resembles a pizza cutter (or, if you are a seamstress, a dart maker).

Measure the length of the wall carefully. If the wall is seven or eight feet tall, you will not have to cut any of the tiles. Mirror tiles are one foot square. A small gap near the ceiling will be covered by the molding. The same applies to the bottom of the wall, but you have more area to fool around with there because the baseboard will cover quite a bit of space. It is not necessary to have the tile meet the floor. But more on reattaching the molding later.

Once you have measured the wall and divided this figure by the length of a tile, you know whether or not any cutting is necessary. Remember, cut the bottom row if you have to cut tiles. Lay out the number needed face side up along the length of the area to be tiled. Using a straightedge (or a metal level) as a guide, run the glass cutter along the predetermined cutting line. Cut through the face of the tile. Then take the tile to a table or counter top that is straight and firm. Place the score line (where you have cut with the glass cutter) on the edge of the table and gently press on the side that overhangs the table. This should snap the glass into two pieces. If you don't have anyone standing by to catch the overhanging piece as it breaks off, be sure to have another table or a high chair for it to fall on. You don't want to break any more tile than is absolutely necessary—for you will break some. (You may be able to talk the dealer who sold you the tile into cutting the tile for you. At least it's worth the try.)

You will need a straight piece of one-by-three-inch lumber, the length of the bottom row of tile. If your wall is long, you may need two or more boards. You will also need a hammer and some long, thin nails. Measure the distance from the ceiling to the floor in one-foot units. Make a line on the wall that the bottom row of tile will rest on.

Lay the board against the wall, with its top against the line you've drawn. Nail the board to the wall; pound the nail in just far enough to hold it to the wall. That's why I recommend long nails. Since the board will be removed after the tile has set, you want enough of the head sticking out to allow easy removal of the nail.

Now, use your level. Lay it on top of the board and be very sure that the bubbles are centered before you insert the next nail. Repeat this procedure all the way along the board. Only in this way will you be assured of an even row of tile. What would be more distracting than looking into a mirror that is set at an angle!

Once the holding board is in place, the rest is easy. Some tile is sold with little self-stick adhesive squares. These are placed on the back of the tile about one-fourth of an inch from each corner and in the center. The tile is then set in place and pressed gently against the wall.

Other tile will need mastic (glue) to attach it to the wall. Purchase this at the same time and place that you obtain the tiles. Ask the dealer to recommend the correct mastic. Apply the mastic on the back at the four corners (but in about one inch from the edge because it will spread) and in the center. The dabs of mastic should be about the size and thickness of a nickel. Do not put the glue close to the edge, or you'll end up with it seeping between the tiles. Is that a mess!

After the first row of tile is in place, put your level on the top edge of the row and make sure it is straight. If not, make any corrections now before the mastic is set. Unless the first row is straight, the entire wall will be off balance.

Continue up the wall, lining up each tile with the one directly below it. Keep using that level, both vertically and horizontally, to insure straight lines. Do not fit the tiles too closely together or the edges may chip. But, don't leave space between them, or the mirror effect will be lost. By taking your time and stepping back from the wall frequently to inspect it, you will be able to see (and correct) any faults while you can still move the tiles.

One hint: in all probability the wall is not exactly even. Pressing all the tiles in with the same amount of pressure could result in a wavy effect. Counteracting this is not difficult. Some mirrors may have to be pressed onto the wall with a little more pressure than others. This will keep the surface of the tile even, and no distortion will occur. That is why it is imperative to step back from the wall and check after each row is applied.

I prefer to use mastic in place of the self-stick adhesive squares because I can adjust the thickness of the mastic more easily. Even if your tile comes with the adhesive squares, you may wish to consider using mastic.

If you tile only a portion of a wall, you will need a cap molding to run down the vertical sides of the tiled area. This can be stained to match the top and bottom moldings. Explain to your lumber dealer what you need, and he will sell you the correct piece for each side. These end pieces, because of their curve, will cover the tile edges even though the tiles extend out from the wall (see Illustration 78).

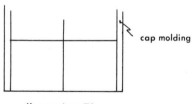

cap molding

Illustration 78

Replace the baseboard, but do not nail it to the wall. Can you imagine what would happen if you tried to put a nail through glass? Instead, use a little adhesive and glue it to the mirrors. The base shoe or quarter round can be nailed back on, but this is tricky, to say the least. You can nail it to the floor, but be careful when swinging that hammer. Again, I suggest glue. The same holds true for the ceiling molding.

Cut the cap moldings so that they fit between the ceiling molding and the baseboard. These are nailed to the wall with finishing nails. Countersink them into the molding, using a nail set. Be sure when nailing that you slant the nails so that they go into the wall and not through the glass. Fill any visible holes with wood putty, which you can stain to match the rest of the wood.

If you tile an entire wall, you will need to use an inside corner molding on either side. This will conceal the unfinished edges of the glass and, more important, the wood trim gives a finished look to the wall. When you install molding at the corners of a room, be sure to drive the nails into the wall adjoining the tiled wall, and not into the glass (see Illustration 79).

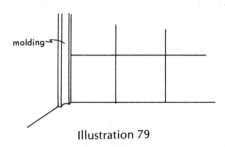

Illustration 79

Another innovation in the home improvement field is fake brick and stone. Because of its light weight it does not need a foundation or extra support, which would be necessary if you were to install real brick. Fake brick can be used in almost any room or decor. The first room that comes to my mind is the family room or den. But think how nice it would look in the kitchen or a bathroom. You could cover a wood planter or use it on bookshelves. Fake brick is waterproof, nonporous, fire retardant, and easy to clean. It does not absorb dirt or grease, and it retains its original color.

There are many reputable manufacturers of fake brick and stone. Their products come in a variety of colors and styles. One style, called "used brick," looks as if it has been scorched. Antique brick, made to look like old, hand-fashioned bricks, is another. Some have textures, variations in color, and irregular edges that make them look authentic.

Another of these fake brick and stone products looks like fieldstone. It can be used indoors or out. Consider using it around a front doorway, in a basement, or in a hallway. The stones are irregular in size and shape, and you make your own pattern as you set them in the mastic. You could even use them in clusters on a painted basement wall to add interest to the room. Another product, fake petrified wood, which is more expensive than plain fake brick, would transform an ordinary living room into a homemaker's pride and joy.

Imitation cork is almost exactly like the real thing—with one great exception. It does not require the upkeep of real cork. It is sealed to prevent dirt and grease from entering the pores, and it is washable. Imitation cork tile is great in a child's room because tacks can be pushed into it without leaving permanent marks. Imitation cork tile comes in twelve-by-twelve-inch squares and is applied to the wall in the same manner as any wall tile. Always make sure that the first row applied is perfectly level and recheck after applying each row in order to maintain that straight line. Because of their light weight, imitation cork tiles will not slip down the wall. Therefore, you will not need a temporary wood base as you did with the mirror tiles.

We've all been in houses that have spindle posts going up a stairway, or used as a divider between living and dining areas, or to give the illusion of an entryway when the front door opens directly into the living room. I once assumed that these were put in when the house was constructed. That isn't true. You can put up your own spindle posts anywhere you like and you don't even need a tool. If you purchase them unfinished, you will need a paintbrush and some stain. You can buy spindle posts already finished, but, naturally, these will be more expensive.

Spindle posts are not limited to just the above uses. You can also use them to construct bookshelves or a coffee table. Maybe you need a stereo center—simple to construct with the correct spindles and shelves. How about a headboard for the guest room or a bookcase headboard for the kids? They can keep a radio, reading lamp, and books on it.

Several manufacturers offer spindles, shelves, and the necessary parts to fasten them together. Some are designed so that you can join a twelve-inch spindle to a fifteen-inch spindle without losing the continuity of the pattern. They come in many styles—Early American, Mediterranean, and Scandinavian, to mention a few.

You may think of a hand-painted mural on a wall as a sign of great wealth. Who can afford to have an artist paint a beautiful picture on a wall? Why not do it yourself? Murals are beautiful on a dining room wall. And consider how a mural would look above a bed in the master bedroom. My sister-in-law painted one above her bed, and it is the focal point of the room. You can also paint Mother Goose scenes in a child's room.

You can purchase wallpaper scenes and hang them exactly as you would regular wallpaper. They are very pretty, but not nearly so impressive as a painted mural. But few of us are artists, so consider the paint-by-number murals available. Directions come with them and differ with the particular manufacturer; so I'll just go lightly over the process.

The wall should be white. Even if the other walls in the room are colored, paint the mural wall white. Not only will it make a nice contrast to the other three walls, but the colors in the mural will not be distorted.

Purchase a kit that has a stenciled pattern and the necessary oil paint to complete the picture. Following the manufacturer's directions, apply the pattern to the wall. Using artist's brushes, follow the numbers and paint the mural. You can even put on a tam and pretend you're Rembrandt! With or without the tam, you'll be proud of the finished product. No need to tell anyone it was done by number—just say that you always had a little bit of the artist in you and now it has found expression!

I have always admired glass-block windows in a bathroom or a basement. We had them in our first house, and I intend to install them in our present one. They allow sunlight to enter the room but no one can see in. Glass blocks are available in clear (although somewhat wavy to the eye) glass. These would not be suitable for a first-floor bathroom, but they would be fine for a basement where natural light is wanted.

Before I describe the installation of glass-block windows, I would like to point out one drawback. You cannot open a glass-block window. Therefore, I do not recommend this type of window for a basement that has only one or two windows and a single stairway. In case of fire, occupants would be trapped, not necessarily by the fire itself but by the smoke. A basement should always have more than one exit. Have one or two windows of ordinary glass which can either be removed or broken in case of an emergency.

Also, you should consider the problem of ventilation. The glass-block window system produced by one manufacturer comes equipped with a small window and screen in the center of the panel. The window opens in, and the screen is on the outside. Pay a little more and have the ventilator system, especially in a bathroom. Even if you already have a ventilation system in the ceiling of the bathroom, there is nothing to equal fresh air.

There is much to be said in favor of glass-block panels. It is almost impossible for a burglar to break through them. Because of their thickness they cannot be broken without a great amount of noise. Since each unit is so small, it would be necessary to break the entire window to make an opening large enough for a human to fit through. You will never need to paint the window sash. Should you have a water seepage problem, the installation of glass block will eliminate it.

If you choose to install glass blocks, measure your window opening exactly. Visit your building materials supplier, see what he has to offer, and ask for the directions for the particular unit you wish to install. A little bit of mortar and your own labor is all that is necessary to have a perfect glass-block window.

Let's not limit ourselves to the inside of the house. Why not take a look outside? Do you have a patio? What a great place to have drinks with neighbors or a picnic supper with your family! Even if you have a very small yard, you can create a patio that will be used on many occasions.

There are many different ways of constructing a patio. Some are complicated and should be done only by a professional. These are the ones that are extremely large or irregular in shape, or that have a four-inch bed of cement poured over wire mesh. You probably could manage the last type, but mixing and pouring cement is a very heavy job and not one I would recommend for a beginner.

I happen to like a patio made out of bricks because it is easy to make, looks very pretty, and is not commonly seen. The first house my husband and I owned had a cement patio that was too small for our needs. The builder had left a large space between the patio and the house. I tried to grow grass in this area, but it always died.

Then I tried ground cover, which also died. Something had to be done to cover this barren space. That's when I hit upon the brick patio idea. Our brick patio tied into an existing one, but there is no reason why you could not construct your own from scratch.

Before you can make a patio, you must determine the area you wish to cover. It's easy to make the space too small. Remember that you will probably want a picnic table and benches, and perhaps a few lawn chairs and tables. Then you'll need room to walk around the furniture without skinning your knees. Be sure that the area is big enough for your needs before you begin construction.

Once you have determined the patio area, measure it out and, using small wood stakes and heavy-duty string, rope off the space. Should grass be growing in the patio area, remove it. Don't try doing this with a shovel. All you will end up with is a bunch of holes all over the place that you will then have to level out—not an easy job by anyone's standards. Instead, rent the tool that is used to remove sod. It works on the same principle as a pizza cutter. You move it in straight lines across the grass and it cuts through the roots. Then you can roll up the grass and use it elsewhere if you want to.

Multiplying the length of the patio times the width will give you the square feet of brick necessary for your job. Bricks differ in size and shape; so be sure to take exact measurements with you when you purchase the brick. Do not be afraid to enter a brickyard designated "wholesale only." Most times you will find that the dealer is more than willing to sell to a home owner. The dealer will tell you how much brick you will need for your particular job. However, be sure to have him mark on your bill of sale that you can return, for full credit, any brick you do not need. Not only does this protect you, but it will decrease the likelihood that he will sell you more than you actually need.

You will also need to purchase a heavy (six millimeter) plastic sheet and ordinary sand in which to set the bricks. The dealer will tell you how much of each you will need when you tell him the measurements of your patio.

Now that the supplies have been purchased and the grass removed, you are ready to start making your patio. First, place a few bricks in the dug-out area to make sure that you have removed enough grass and dirt to accommodate a two-inch bed of sand under the bricks. The bricks should be fairly even with the surrounding grass. True, the patio can be above the grass line, but then you will need to hand trim the grass that borders the patio.

Do not set the bricks below grass level or water will stand on the patio after any rain. It is best to gently slope the patio from the house to the grass line, with the bricks at the outer edge about one-half inch above ground level. This allows for drainage, and you will not have the problem of having to hand trim the grass.

If any excess dirt must be removed, do it now. Then, using the back side of a rake, even out the terrain, remembering to slope away from the foundation of the house.

Now spread the plastic sheet, cutting it to fit the patio area. The plastic prevents the sand from sinking into the ground and, with it, your entire patio. Then spread most of the sand over the area. Using your garden hose (with the fine nozzle—who needs sand all over the place!), wet down the sand thoroughly. Allow it to dry out and then repeat the procedure. The idea is to set the sand so that it will not sink when you lay the bricks. One final wetting down should accomplish the trick.

It will be necessary to tamp (smooth or flatten out) the sand. You can accomplish this with the help of a two-by-four. Start at the foundation line and pull the board towards the edge of the patio, sloping the area gradually downward. You can do this very easily by attaching a string to both ends of the board and then pulling the board toward you and away from the house.

Time now to set the bricks. Maybe you just want to place them in straight lines, or perhaps you are inventive and wish to stagger them to form an irregular pattern. That decision is yours. Regardless of the pattern you choose, do not leave much room between the bricks. Otherwise your furniture will sink between them or a woman in high heels may trip and fall. So, butt them together as closely as possible.

Push the bricks into the sand with a gentle twisting motion. They need not go all the way into the sand—just far enough to hold them in place. But make sure that the surfaces are level with each other, or the patio will be uneven.

After the bricks are set in the sand, you will need to spread a coat of sand over the entire patio. Again, using the finest setting on the nozzle of your hose, spray the sand into the spaces between the bricks. Wait one or two days for the sand to thoroughly dry out and repeat the spraying. (You may need extra sand, depending upon the space between the bricks and the atmospheric moisture.)

Wash off any excess sand, remove the wooden sticks and string, and you have a beautiful patio. Invite the neighbors over for cocktails and glory in the compliments you will receive.

Now, back to the inside of your house. We all need bookshelves somewhere in the house. I chose the den for my collection of books, but I realized that the children also needed room to store their encyclopedias, dictionaries, and other books. My youngest daughter also wanted a place to display her collection of beer cans (would you believe it?).

In the section on the many uses of spindle posts, I suggested one way to build a bookcase. Now I offer another way.

Most building material dealers sell shelf standards and brackets. Standards are the pieces of metal that are attached to the wall with screws. These pieces have vertical slots in them so you can position the shelf brackets (the pieces of metal that support the shelf) at any level you need, for either large or small books. One possible placement of the shelves is shown in Illustration 80. Your own needs will dictate the space between the shelves.

You can purchase unfinished boards and finish them to your liking. Or you can buy prefinished shelves. Another idea I'd like to suggest is the use of glass shelves. They are beautiful, and because they are clear, they give a feeling of spaciousness. We wanted them in the den and in our girl's bedroom. Purchasing these shelves from a glass store is a very expensive proposition. Each shelf, since to support books, must be three-sixteenths inch or

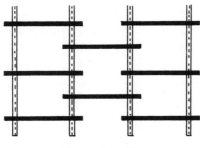

Illustration 80

one-fourth inch thick, and it must be rounded at the edges.

Not wishing to spend a lot of money, I watched the local advertisements for a store going out of business—fixtures and all. The store I found was the local dime store. I was able to buy glass display and divider shelves (sixteen in all) for fifteen cents each. Most towns have a store going out of business at some time. Using these shelves and purchasing the standards and brackets at the local discount store saved a bundle of money. But, more important, they are a fine addition to the room.

Too often we tend to think of window treatment only in terms of drapes or curtains. Have you ever considered shutters? In a colonial-style house, they can be used in any room. But even in a modern or traditional house, they can be used in a bathroom, a powder room, or a bedroom. They can be closed to shut out light. You can open one or two sections if you wish to allow light and air to enter, or you can fold back the entire unit to achieve an open window area.

When measuring for window shutters, you must be

most accurate. There are two different ways of installing shutters. You might want them attached inside the frame (casing) of the window, or you might want them to cover the entire window frame. Only you can decide what best suits your purpose. Either way, make exact measurements of the area to be covered. Should you choose an inside mounting, you would measure according to Illustration 81. An outside mounting is determined as shown in Illustration 82.

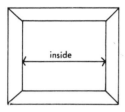

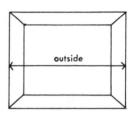

Illustration 81   Illustration 82

Fortunately, even most men are reluctant to install window shutters without professional help. So imagine what a feather in your cap it will be when you hang them yourself. The secret lies in purchasing shutters that already have the hanging hinges attached to them by means of another strip that has the adjoining hinge affixed to it. All that is necessary is to nail the strip to the window casing (frame) and insert the pins that hold the shutter in place.

If you wish the panels to fold back, you will need an extra hardware unit for use between panels. This is called the interpanel hinge and allows for full movement when there are two or more panels on one side.

Should the molding around your window be curved, you can still use the hanging strips. Just nail the strip on so that the side facing you is tight to the molding. Don't worry about the small gap behind—no one is going to see it. You can insert small pieces of wood (shims) behind the strip to keep it from pulling out from the molding, but this really isn't necessary.

You will need to purchase knobs that screw in so that you can open and shut the shutters. You might also want a latch set. This looks like the hook and eye locking device on old screen doors. It allows the shutters to be locked from the inside—not only to deter burglars but also to prevent the shutters from flying open if the window is open and the wind is high. If you use the latch set, it must be mounted at least two inches from the knobs.

One of the most overlooked areas is the garage. Tools are strewn all over the floor; lawn care tools and equipment lean against the wall. With all the things one manages to store in a garage, it's a wonder that there's room for the car!

In a previous chapter, I touched briefly on the various uses of pegboard. Remember? Pegboard is hardboard that has little holes in it for hooks and shelves. If you have pegboard on your garage wall, you will be able to hang up the garden tools, brooms, shovels, sleds, sweepers, and all the rest of the paraphernalia. Summer lawn chairs can be hung, as well as ladders. Just be sure to use heavy-duty hooks for heavy items. Heavy-duty hooks are used with the pegboard that has the large holes (see Illustration 83).

The use of pegboard is certainly not limited to the garage. You have acquired a variety of tools, so you will need a place to keep them, a place that is safely away from little children who could get hurt, but still easily accessible to you. What better place than a wall in the utility room? A shelf takes care of the level, hooks will hold the hammer, and pinch-type clips will hold screwdrivers and nail set.

Nail heavy-duty pegboard onto the wall above your

washing machine, install some shelves, and you have a place to store detergent and bleach. Even your iron can

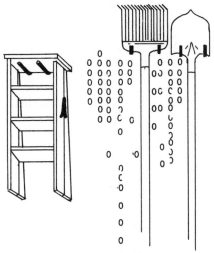

Illustration 83

rest safely on such a shelf. Or try using pegboard in the broom closet. By hanging up the wet mop, the dust mop, and the broom, you avoid a clutter on the floor.

Any woman who sews knows that there is nothing more annoying than having to go through the thread box each time she needs a different color—not to mention the aggravation of trying to locate scissors and bobbins. By hanging pegboard above the sewing area you can eliminate these problems. Each spool of thread can be stuck on its own peg, scissors can be hung up, and bobbins can be kept in baby food jars, held to the pegboard by spring attachment hooks. You can even drill a hole through your yardstick and hang it up. I suggest draping the entire unit with a thin piece of plastic. This keeps dust from gathering on the spools of thread. Just throw the sheet of plastic over the top of the pegboard and everything will be protected.

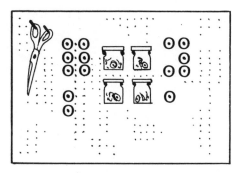

Illustration 84

I hope that now you will never be afraid to tackle a home remodeling project. Nothing is impossible if you want to accomplish it. Hopefully, with the help of this book you can transform your house into the house of your dreams.

Index